MW01614762

SOUL
SEEKER

SOUL
SEEKER

A Journey To Discover—Who Am I
& What Is My Higher Purpose?

CINDY REYNOLDS

ENDLESS PULSE, LLC

ISBN (paperback): 978-1-7375237-0-3
ISBN (ebook): 978-1-7375237-1-0

Editing: Doug Childers; Valerie Costas
Cover Design: *the*BookDesigners
Cover Image: Shutterstock.com
Interior design: Christy Day, Constellation Book Services
Author Photo: Phil Channing

Printed in the United States of America

Dedication

To the Beings of Light who guide us and
protect us on our path through life.
Thank you!

To my daughter, Tamarin, whose love and light shines bright
from the "Temple in the Sky." I am so grateful for you!

And to Soul Seekers everywhere, may the light of our
eternal Self show us the way each and every day!

CONTENTS

Introduction

Have you ever had experiences that offered no logical explanation? Have you witnessed a phenomenon that if you were to describe it to others, they might think you were crazy? Or maybe you've stayed in quiet conflict, and wondered why these extraordinary events happen to you?

Do you ever consider the possibility that even after a loved one passes, he or she can still see you, be with you, and yes, intelligently communicate with you—Soul to Soul? Do you believe that what we call death is not the end at all, but the beginning of a new life cycle?

If so, you are not alone. Worldwide Research studies show that millions of people believe in life after death. Moreover, one in ten people have had an out-of-body experience (OBE). In the United States alone, it is estimated that 200,000 people a year have had a near death experience (NDE), and that six out of ten grieving people have heard or seen a departed loved one and acknowledged an after-death communication (ADC).

I have experienced many of these phenomena, and they have changed the course of my life.

When a loved one dies, we grieve for our loss. The thought of never seeing them, being with them, hugging them, or hearing their voice again can be an unbearably painful experience.

Yet in dreams, we often see them and speak with them. We can also witness extraordinary events and synchronistic phenomena that signify their presence—or, because we are not taught that such occurrences are possible, we may not even notice these manifestations when they happen.

Such other-worldly experiences can be tremendously healing. However, a July 4th 2017 article in *Psychology Today* on "The Healing Effects of After-Death Communication" reported that many people keep such experiences a secret, fearing they will be thought of as crazy.

I know I did!

Many cultures accept after-death presence (ADP) as perfectly normal. Traditionally, our culture has not. However, many of us continue to believe that, even after death, our relationships grow, and that our loved ones never leave us or forget us.

When I experienced my first after-death presence as a teen, followed by an out-of-body experience as a young adult, it didn't make any sense. Why me? I was an ordinary girl from Los Angeles. I was not a medium, a clairvoyant, or a psychic. These events just happened and, not having anyone I could talk to, I felt isolated and alone.

As a result, I've had an overwhelming desire to write about these phenomena and bring normalcy to them. I am happy to say that in recent years, awareness of after-death presence and after-death communication has come to the forefront of Western culture, and countless spiritual/new age books are now available.

My firsthand experiences have led me to conclude that death is not the end of our existence, and our Souls are eternal.

Most importantly, this same eternal Soul lives within each of us—right here, right now. It is a guiding force. Its intelligence and enlightened presence are always there, not only while deep in meditation or at spiritual retreats, but in every moment, especially during difficult times.

When darkness plunges us into deep states of fear, pain, or grief, and life feels unbearable, we may surrender and let go of everything we have been holding onto. In this vulnerable state we often find ourselves in the presence of a source of strength, power, and wisdom that resides within us. That source, by whatever name you call it—the Soul, the higher self as defined by the new age movement, or the Hindu Atman, to name a few—has been a saving light in the darkness for countless human beings since time immemorial.

This has been my own experience, as well.

At an early age, tragic events launched me on the path of a seeker. The more questions I asked and the more I prayed for strength, the more doorways opened within, expanding my vision and worldview. I unwittingly discovered a place of power within and learned to tune into my Soul's higher voice.

Insights and energy flowed through me in a process of transformation that built bridges to my Soul and provided tools to turn fear into trust, insecurity into confidence, and hopelessness into faith—even while faced with unthinkable tragedies.

When deceased loved ones appeared to me as a teenager, it was often with prophetic messages that confirmed I was anything but crazy.

A trauma-induced out-of-body-experience as an adult taught me to utilize the fear-based thoughts and emotions of my human personality to uncover the contents of my own Soul plan and practice Soul growth.

It's the terrible tragedies and devastating challenges in life that offer us the most remarkable opportunities to gain higher more enlightened perspectives and evolve to become a healing presence in the world. This is the goal of the Soul's journey into the physical realm.

After my daughter's mild traumatic brain injury and misdiagnosis, I learned to read the electrical activity of brainwaves and became a certified QEEG Technologist.

I started my own company, NeuroFit® Marin, to address the need for personalized brain training and NeuroFitness awareness. Knowing how our thoughts etch neuropathways in the brain for good or ill, I also became a Soul Coach and created the Soulercise® Mind Fitness program which, for over a decade, has incorporated the transforming voice of the Soul I had found into a universal healing process.

SOUL SEEKER expounds on the notion that Soul fitness is as important as body fitness, and the seeming threshold of death does not separate Souls who inhabit bodies from Souls who have moved beyond the limits of the physical world.

It also offers insights into age-old questions such as: "Who am I?" "Why am I here?" "What is my higher purpose?"

As a teaching memoir, *Soul Seeker* focuses on key moments in my life—moments that paved a pathway of self-discovery and enlightenment that can apply to us all. The devastating events and extraordinary experiences I share will teach you how to Soulercise—to tune in to your Soul's voice and transform thoughts and emotions into a higher vibrational mindset.

As you read my story, what you learn can be applied to the challenging situations in your own life. You will learn new terms and truths, and each will have personal meaning.

My deepest wish is to help you develop an increasingly tangible, life-changing relationship with your own Soul. For when your Soul becomes a guiding light in your life, and its whispering voice becomes as close and familiar as the sound of your own breath, you have crossed a bridge where two seemingly separate worlds become one.

Then your Soul, with all its light, wisdom, and enlightenment, operates within you wherever you go, and you become a healing presence in the world.

It's an honor to share my story with you.

PART 1
A PLACE
OF POWER
WITHIN

CHAPTER 1

The Journey Begins

It was a hot August morning in Carmel, California. My younger sister, Debby, and I had spent the last three weeks training and competing in tennis matches at the John Gardiner Tennis Ranch in Carmel Valley, California. Now it was graduation day.

I stood before the mirror in our one-room cabin excited to finally be wearing my new white tennis dress with red piping down the front. Saved for this special day, it fit perfectly. For an eager 12-year-old athlete with a sense of style, it didn't get any better than this.

Absorbed in my impromptu fashion show, I hardly noticed, or chose to ignore, the knock on our door. Debby sat on her bed nursing a tennis injury—a very sore ankle that required constant soaking. I turned back and forth in front of the mirror, viewing my dress from every possible angle.

Then a second, more powerful knock penetrated my fantasy world. In high spirits, I clasped the red barrette that kept my long blonde bangs from falling in my eyes and practically skipped over to open the door.

Jenny, our camp counselor, stood there, it seemed uncomfortably. Usually cheerful, she now had a strange look on her thin, sun-weathered face while saying, "Cindy, you and Debby need to come to the main office right away. Your parents are on the phone."

"Is something wrong," I asked?

"They want to talk to you," was all she would say.

My parents had driven to Carmel from Los Angeles with close family friends, the Griers, to play golf and attend our graduation. They were supposed to be here any minute, so I didn't understand why they were calling us on the phone.

It was a long walk to the office. We passed by rows of white wooden chairs blanketing the tennis courts and saw the grand podium where later that day we would receive our well-deserved certificates. My excitement over graduating, at a fever-pitch only moments ago, had now given way to feelings of uncertainty and a vague apprehension.

"Was something wrong?" I wondered silently as Debby and I entered the office, the screen door banging closed loudly behind us.

Mom's concerned voice greeted me over the phone as she said, "Cindy, we're really sorry, but your father and I had to return home. He had a sudden business matter to deal with. I'm afraid we won't be able to be there with you girls for your graduation."

Rather than being reassured, the anxious feeling only deepened. My father had never before had any business emergency of which I was aware.

"What kind of business matter?" I asked.

Mom attempted an explanation, but it sounded awkward and did not make sense to me. For a split second, I wondered if my parents were making all this up. Ultimately, I accepted their explanation and tried desperately to process my disappointment. Then Mom asked to speak to Debby, and I handed my sister the phone. Debby also grimaced in disappointment at the news that Mom and Dad would not be attending our graduation. Her long brown hair framed a now sullen face, and her brown eyes reflected the deep pain we both felt.

Exchanging a look of sadness, we silently shared our heartfelt regret. Only eighteen months apart, our closeness was comforting, but this special day wouldn't be the same without Mom and Dad.

When Debby hung up, we returned to our cabin, walking glumly down the path between the empty tennis courts, now oblivious to the rows of white wooden chairs and the podium where we would soon receive our graduation certificates.

I wasn't walking fast, yet I noticed that Debby was having a tough time keeping up with me. Remembering that she had a sore ankle and knowing she probably didn't want to make a big deal about it, I slowed down and turned to give her a quick hug without saying a word of concern.

We had both endured the same long grueling hours of training over the previous three weeks. Debby was not as athletically inclined as I was, so I assumed the training had strained her ankle. The fleeting thought that something else was wrong with Debby passed through my mind, only to be washed away by the heartache of our parents' absence.

Our family was close, and we always had a lot of fun together. My dad, Byron Stuart Reynolds Jr., or Bob, Bo, or Bobo as he was called, grew up in Los Angeles. He worked at Bandini, a fertilizer company founded in 1927 by my great grandfather, Thomas

Stuart Reynolds, and my grandfather, Byron Stuart Reynolds Sr. The company was named after Bandini Blvd., where both the business resided and the manufacturing plant with giant mounds of manure piled high along the property. There was no doubt that we always had the best-looking front lawn in the neighborhood. My dad was famous for annually seeding and fertilizing it to a beautiful emerald-green color.

My mom, Genevieve McIntosh Reynolds, or Vevie as she was affectionately called, moved to Los Angeles from Dallas with my grandmother, Bettye, shortly after her father was suddenly killed in a car accident when she was 11 years old. Mom attended the private high school, Westlake, and then went to college at USC where my parents met. She was an active member of her sorority and a dear friend to many. Dad was active in his fraternity and together they made a wonderful team.

Mom and Dad were married in their early twenties and eventually moved with a group of their friends from USC to a suburb of Los Angeles known as Hancock Park. They all had kids around the same time, so we grew up having known each other since we were in our mothers' bellies. Our families were all close. At one point my parents and several friends got together and bought a plot of land in the middle of Palm Desert. They called it "Los Conejos" and built 12 houses around a pool, where we would all go several times a year to vacation.

My parents always knew how to have fun, so without them at our graduation ceremony it was not a memorable event. Afterwards, we caught a ride home with the Griers. I was quiet in the car, staring out the window and trying to process the random thoughts running through my mind. I had a nagging feeling that my dad hadn't gone on a business trip. Intuitively, I knew something was wrong. But I didn't know what, and I kept my fears to myself on the long ride back to Los Angeles.

When we arrived home that evening, our parents greeted us at the door. Mom's usually stylish blond hair was disheveled. Her attractive, Romanesque features seemed contorted, and her expressive and usually glowing blue eyes looked pained. Dad gave me a hug, but his normally warm embrace now felt distant. The cheerful smile that usually lit up his face when he looked at me was noticeably absent, and his hazel brown eyes seemed to avoid mine.

I could feel that something terrible had happened. When we entered the house, I saw flowers everywhere—in the entrance hall, the living room, and the den.

"Why are all these flowers here?" I asked, though I instinctively feared the answer.

"Girls come into the den and sit down," my dad said.

We went into the den, and my parents sat next to us on the couch. I remembered wondering if the dog had died. It was almost a hopeful thought in retrospect, as if I were unconsciously hoping for a tragedy of manageable proportions. But as is so often the case in life, such choices are not ours to make.

"Girls," Mom said somberly. "Your grandmother, Janet (pronounced Jeanette), was killed in a car accident a few nights ago. She and Honey (our affectionate name for my grandfather) were driving home from a dinner party just a few blocks away. Two teenagers were drag racing up over the small hill on 3rd Street and one of them smashed into the side of Honey's car as he made the turn onto Rimpau. Janet was thrown from the car and killed instantly. Honey is in the hospital, but he's going to be all right."

I was stunned. It was incomprehensible. Janet, my loving

grandmother, was gone...forever. Janet, who gave Debby and me each a space of our own in her backyard to plant flowers; who taught us to make cookies and custard; who had sewed us dresses since we were little girls; who had only last week sent letters and care packages with candy and goodies to us at tennis camp.

Our entire lives had been lived in her blessed presence, baking with her in her kitchen, playing dress-up in her clothes, often sleeping over with her and Honey. Janet had always been there for us and made time for us. Now she was gone. We would never see her again, ever. And my father was never going to see his mother again.

I looked over at Dad, and his loving eyes finally met mine. They were welling up with tears, full of an inexpressible grief. I suddenly felt his deep loss, and I, too, began to cry.

Mom and Dad spent the rest of the evening with us, answering all our questions and making sure we were all right. The depth of our family bond gave Debby and me the resources to bear a tragedy whose magnitude our young minds could not assimilate.

The funeral had taken place that afternoon. My parents told us they hadn't wanted to ruin our graduation ceremony. I understood, but the graduation had been spoiled. Both the camp counselors and the Griers had known about our grandmother's death, and I had sensed the hidden truth in them.

I also felt that because my mom had lost her father at such a young age, this had influenced my parents' decision not to bring us home early. But I wished I could have said goodbye to Janet. I wished I could have attended her funeral.

Debby and I were exhausted, so our parents took us upstairs and tucked us into bed, each in our own rooms. Afterward, I lay in the darkness, my 12-year-old mind haunted by thoughts and images of my grandmother's death. Nestled in my cocoon of soft sheets and a navy velvet comforter, I cried for what seemed like hours, lying in a strange limbo far from my ordinary self.

I prayed from the depths of my being to find the strength to cope with this shocking tragedy. I wondered: "Where do we go when we die? Is Janet still near me? Can she hear me if I call out to her?"

More than just thoughts, they were deep reflections that sent tingling sensations running through my whole body. An overwhelming need to know the answers to these questions leapt through me. I had to say goodbye to my grandmother. But she was gone, and I didn't know what to do.

My distress increased, until finally, adamantly, I told myself, "Well, since I couldn't say goodbye to Janet at her funeral, I'm going to say goodbye right here!"

Eyes closed; I saw her in my mind. Her coifed red hair was as beautiful as ever, and even the faint freckles covering her barely five-foot-two elegant frame looked as real as the last day I saw her. Of course, she was wearing a sun dress. Janet hardly ever wore pants.

With a vision of Janet now clear in my mind, a vivid feeling of her presence enveloped me. I reached my arms out and virtually hugged her warm and loving image with all my might. It was all quite spontaneous, yet so utterly powerful. An astounding place of power that had no name opened within me. It allowed the blessed bond of our love, strong but shaken, to be reborn beyond time and space. A sense of peace and consolation replaced my pain and sadness.

Intuition is a powerful force. And even in the face of incredible tragedy, there is a place within where you can find peace.

Without another thought, I fell asleep fully at peace in my grandmother's loving embrace.

Overwhelmed by the tragedy of Janet's death, and grieving for Honey, our family was in deep mourning. We were very worried about Honey, and not just physically. He and Janet had been married for 40 years, and the shock of their violent separation, and its finality, was a terrible blow.

Then, within a week of our return from tennis camp, our family was once again thrown into sudden turmoil.

Huge red blotches began to appear on Debby's legs, and soon the pain in her ankle became a daily challenge. It finally reached the point where Debby tried to find some relief in the bathtub but then couldn't walk back to her room. Dad had to carry her, crying in pain from the weight of her ankle dangling against his arm. I watched helplessly as my parents tried everything to relieve her discomfort—to no avail.

Debby and I were not only close in age, but we also genuinely loved one another. We shared many of the same friends as kids and liked to ride our Sting Ray bikes around the neighborhood. We often played games or watched TV together on weekends or when Mom and Dad were out for the evening during the week. We loved to spend the night at our grandmother Bettye's house, playing on the swan float in her pool or riding to town in her six-ties-style Cadillac—probably hoping for candy at Wil Wright's. Debby and I always kept each other company, laughing at our private jokes on long drives to Palm Springs or when travelling to Newport Beach for summer vacations. So now seeing Debby in so much pain was truly terrifying.

While at tennis camp, we had thought Debby's condition was sports-related, as the camp counselors had said. Now it seemed like something much more serious. Mom and Dad called the doctor late that night, and he came to our house to examine Debby. Afterwards, he and my parents went into the den and closed the sliding wooden door to talk. Scared to death, I wandered aimlessly alone in the hallway outside. A few minutes later the door slid open, it seemed in slow motion, and Dad called me inside. The mood in the room was somber.

"Cindy, we're taking Debby to the hospital," Mom said. "The doctor doesn't know what's wrong with her. She's going to stay there for a few days under observation."

I could find no words. Tragedy had been swirling around us since our return home. I knew now that our family was no longer safe from the worst the world might bring. Perhaps we never had been. And I couldn't help fearing that something terrible might now befall my little sister.

Debby's hospital stay stretched from several days to many weeks. The doctors were baffled by her condition. Every day after school I went to stay with my godparents, Jeanne and Dick, who lived two blocks from our house.

One night Mom and Dad came later than usual to pick me up on their way back from the Children's Hospital. I saw something new in their faces, a heaviness that hadn't been there the day before. Their silence in the car on the way home was painfully nerve-wracking. It felt like that long walk from the tennis camp office back to the cabin; I was carrying a feeling of dread that I could not make go away.

Dad parked the car in the front of the house. We came slowly up the brick walkway to the front door, and Dad put the key in the lock.

Then Mom turned to me and said with a great deal of pain, "Cindy, the doctor told us tonight that Debby doesn't have long to live. She has an incurable blood disease. They're doing everything they can to find medicine to save her."

Mom's softly spoken words hit me with shattering force. It was more heartache than my body could bear, and more agony than my mind could endure. My sister was going to die, but she was only 10 years old. She was my best friend. I loved her so much. How could she die, and I keep on living? Janet...and now Debby? But...why? At that moment, my life changed forever. Mercifully, I went into shock.

CHAPTER 2

The Art of Coping

It was not only my life that changed. All of our lives had changed. Debby did not die as the doctors had predicted. She hung on, with determination, medical help, and our love. The weeks became months in isolation, endless blood tests and exhaustive research as a team of doctors at Children's Hospital treated her mysterious illness as best as they could while they sought to discover its exact nature.

Eventually, the doctors were able to manage her illness with a newly introduced treatment of Cortisone/corticosteroids. She was one of the first groups of people to be diagnosed with Lupus in the modern era, and one of the first patients to be treated for this disease for which there is still no known cure.

For the first year after her diagnosis, Debby was in the hospital more than she was out. Eventually, the doctors were able to treat Debby as an out-patient most of the time. However, she did have flare-ups over the years that sent her back into the hospital for treatment. During those times, Mom spent most of her day there with Debby, and Dad usually went to the hospital on weekends and sometimes after work. During the first year of Debby's hospitalization, I often stayed with Jeanne and Dick, and I talked on the phone with Mom and Debby every day after school.

In these difficult and uncertain years of not knowing whether Debby would live or die, I felt so alone. Once again, my only recourse was an impulse to pray.

After Janet's death, I simply prayed within for the strength to cope. But this time, I consciously reached out to something beyond for help. We had always gone to church as kids, but church then had meant sitting in the balcony, whispering, or passing notes, and going out for donuts afterwards. During those hospital years, as soon as I hung up the phone after my daily chat with Mom and Debby, I found myself praying, long and hard, to an unknown external source for help.

In those moments of prayer, an indescribable feeling of safety and comfort once again surrounded me. This time, my childlike hope, which grew into faith, was that the sincerity and intensity of my prayers would also be transmuted into a source of help for Debby. I had no doubt that my prayers were being heard.

Again, I had found a powerful place within that had no name, where I could take refuge and find peace. In my innocence, I had also unwittingly tapped into that spiritual, intelligent, and unseen force that listens and assists us in our time of need. But I never discussed these feelings with anyone.

Debby's deep and quiet courage as she coped with her childhood ordeal, and the traumatic impact her disease had on her, was a profound and ongoing lesson that challenged me and taught me more than I could have imagined.

I vividly remember in the first year of her hospitalization when she was finally allowed to come home to spend Easter Sunday with our family. I hadn't visited her at all because it was hospital rules that you had to be 16 years old to visit the third-floor ward where Debby lived. I was excited when I arrived at the hospital with my parents to pick her up and waited anxiously in the lobby for Debby to arrive in the elevator.

Nothing could have prepared me for what I saw when the elevator door opened.

Debby's face was swollen three times its size, a side-effect of her medication. It was a different era, and it wasn't common for our family to sit down and talk. And even if we had, it may have been impossible to comprehend the full extent of the change in her appearance.

I tried my best to disguise the shock of what she looked like. Debby wore a white knit Easter dress, and a blue ribbon adorned her beautiful long brown hair. But her eyes were practically buried within her swollen flushed cheeks. And yet, as she walked over to greet me, Debby carried herself with a palpable sense of strength and confidence.

Despite all of her pain and suffering, with all the drugs and tests and her separation from home and family, Debby never let Lupus define her. She was resilient and continued on in life with the heart of a champion. Each time Debby was released from the hospital, she consistently demonstrated love, strength, and grace—never seeking attention or succumbing to the trials of her illness. And she always shared the avalanche of candy, flowers, and comics that had been given to her by family and friends. We spent hours on our parents' bed eating candy and reading comics, laughing, and watching TV together.

One time Debby came home and apologized profusely for not having any comic books or candy. It was then that I noticed her compassion. She had given her comic books to a little boy who was in quarantine, and they had to be burned after he read them.

Debby also told me about another little boy whose mother had abandoned him. He suffered from a large tumor-like growth which had severely deformed his head. His room was right across the hall from Debby's, and when Mom was visiting, she would always stop in and say hi to him. The nurses told Debby that Mom was the only person he didn't hide his face from. Her example of compassion influenced Debby, and before being discharged, she sent the little boy all of her candy. Debby showed me that no matter how much we suffer, we always have room in our hearts to care for others.

Over the years, one of the hardest things for both of us to endure was the cruelty of the kids at public school.

Due to her lengthy hospital stays, Debby was required to finish the current school year at the local public school, then stay back a year and return to private school with all our friends. During her rare appearance at public school, the kids there continually taunted and teased her about her swollen face, often following her home from school and laughing at her, calling her chipmunk.

This killed me. There was little I could do to protect her. Yet Debby never, ever complained. Her strength was impeccable in the face of the torments and trials she endured.

School was not going much better for me either. Raised in a nice, upper-middle class Los Angeles home and attending a private school, I wanted the life my parents wished for me—good grades, a social life, high school graduation, to go on to USC, join a sorority, date, go to football games, and after that a conventional marriage and a traditional life.

By the time 7th grade rolled around, however, new feelings began to surface, and the life I thought I had wanted no longer seemed to fit who I was becoming. Too much had happened for me not to be changed. My grandmother had died in a car accident three blocks from our house. I had been told that my little sister was going to die of an incurable blood disease, and with my parents practically living at the hospital, it was as if I had lost them, too. I was spending most of my time living with my godparents and coping as best I could.

In school I was constantly being told by my teachers that I wasn't applying myself, that I daydreamed too much, that I wasn't living up to my potential. Yes, I was daydreaming. I would sit in class and doodle with my pencil, look out the window and wonder—where do we go when we die? Are we alone? Who was the first person to ever be born, the very first person? Where did he or she come from? Do we have a Soul? What is it exactly, and where does it go when we die?

These daydreams that occupied me led to more frustration. No one that I knew, not my family, not my teachers, and certainly not my friends, could answer these questions. So, I buried them inside and tried to get good grades so I could go to a good college, so I could succeed and have the life I thought I was supposed to have.

Success eluded me. The two years after Janet's death and Debby's illness had been full of stress, struggle, and confusion. I was miserable in the private school system with its strict, uncreative learning methodologies, its institutional atmosphere of petty rules and regulations, its checks towards detention for various infractions such as out-of-uniform or out-of-supplies. For some reason, I never had the right supplies for class and there always seemed to be something wrong with my uniform. I couldn't seem to fit in anywhere.

Truthfully, it was a fabulous college preparatory school, but I was a lost spirit needing to be prepared for life. I needed food for my Soul as well as my mind. Something inside me, a voice I trusted more and more, told me I was in the wrong place. My Soul felt agitated in this claustrophobic environment. Unable to apply myself, as my teachers kept insisting, my grades suffered accordingly.

When a particularly bad progress report arrived the fall of my sophomore year, Mom and Dad sat with me in Dad's study and listened to my unending pleas to attend Fairfax High School with my boyfriend. But Fairfax was out of our district, and my parents would have to lie about our address to get me in. More importantly, they knew that going to public school to be with my boyfriend was no reason to pull me away from one of the best educations in L.A.

Finally, to my shock and relief, the principal expelled me for breaking the honor code. My parents were understandably upset, but sympathetic to my situation. They researched alternative private schools and decided to send me to Argyll Academy, a small private girls' school in North Hollywood. Now 15 years old, and Argyll student number 52, I felt like a hopeless failure. That was when the universe stepped in and delivered my first mentor.

CHAPTER 3

Three Soulful Questions

I arrived at Argyll in the middle of the semester, but quickly made friends with the in-crowd. Social adaptation was not an issue for me. After only a month, however, concerned teachers once again complained about my lack of attention to my work. Apparently applying myself was still a problem. Mrs. Althauser, or Mrs. A as we called her, was the school principal monitoring the new kid, and early one morning she called me into her office.

Even as the principal she wore our school uniform, a tartan skirt, white shirt, and gray blazer. Her boyish short gray hair capped her six-foot thick frame, and her piercing blue eyes commanded my attention.

"Cindy, I have been keeping an eye on you," she said intently and then continued. "I can tell you have a lot of potential, and I want to do everything in my power to help you succeed here. If there is anything you need, help with assignments or personal matters, anything at all just let me know. My door is always open, but it is up to you to walk in."

I was shocked. The principal actually wanted to help me. She didn't reprimand me. In fact, she actually instilled a sense of hope within me.

Always motivated by a challenge, I took her up on the offer. One day, the vision of myself as a lost Soul with no one to turn to, spun my emotions out of control. Confused and crying, I couldn't go to class. I needed help, and I knew it. Mrs. A had said it was up to me to walk into her office, and that I could come anytime I needed anything. So, I took her at her word.

She stood like a towering statue behind her desk and told me to sit down in the green leather chair next to the window. She came around to stand beside me, and the intensity of her presence was unnerving. When I couldn't stop crying, she grabbed my chin, forcing me to look straight into her crystal blue eyes.

"Who are you?" she asked.

I was shocked into silence. I didn't know what she meant. When I tried to mumble something in response, she silenced me.

"Be quiet, Cindy. Don't tell me now. I want you to go home this afternoon and really ask yourself—who am I? Then write down in one sentence the clearest answer that comes to you."

I went home that afternoon and worked on this exercise with more conviction than any homework assignment I had ever done. Just asking one simple question sent me deeper into myself than I had ever gone.

To my amazement, I discovered a great truth. I had been asking meaningful questions for several years. But until that afternoon I had always looked outside of myself for the answers. It never occurred to me to look for the answers in the same place the questions came from—inside of me.

Still not quite certain how to find the correct answer, I turned on my record player and sat on the bed. I took a moment to close my eyes, to really ask the question, "Who am I?"

At first, I wasn't quite sure that I knew. As I continued asking, answers rose to the surface of my mind. The first answer that came was, "I am Cindy."

"But who was Cindy?" I thought harder and deeper. Then another answer came. This one I wrote down.

"I am a person in search of meaning in the chaos of my life."

This seemed the truest answer to the question Mrs. A had posed. I felt there must be some meaning in the terrible events of the past few years, and I wanted to know what that meaning was. That was what my questions about the Soul, life, and death had been aimed at all along.

The next day I took my sentence back to Mrs. A. When she read it, she looked up at me and I could see that she was pleased. Her ice blue eyes were full of warmth.

"Very good, Cindy," she said. "Now that you've told me who you are, I want to know why you are here. I want you to go home today and really think about this, really ask yourself—why am I here? And when the answer comes to you, write it down in one sentence and bring it back to me."

It seemed like a weird question. But it also seemed like a great challenge. I knew this was not a game we were playing; it was a spiritual quest.

That afternoon I went home, shut myself in my bedroom, and put on my favorite album, *The Doors*. Before, when I was alone and wondering about life, listening to music, I really was just daydreaming, following my thoughts and questions at random without a sense of purpose, not really expecting to find an answer. But this was different. Now I was really thinking. Now I was looking within myself for an answer that I intuitively knew was there, and I was determined to find it.

"Why am I here?" I earnestly asked myself, trying to reach beyond a shallow response. The first answer that came was mundane.

"I am here to study in order to go to a good college."

But this wasn't quite it. College was over two years in the future. Why was I here now? I knew I was trying to discover something important, something deeper and more real than studying for college. After letting my immediate thoughts settle for a moment, another answer came that felt truer.

I wrote down, "I am in school learning to know who I am."

"Good, Cindy," Mrs. A said when she read it the next day. "Now, I have one more question for you. I want you to go home and really ask yourself—what is my higher purpose? I want you to think about this and write down the answer that comes."

Once again, I locked myself in my room after school, turned on the music and began contemplating my new question. I was excited that my daydreaming was now actually creative, purposeful inquiry. Such questions had always spontaneously emerged in me, but now someone was guiding me to look within myself. My random thoughts now had a focus, triggering deeper answers from within me that seemed to change my sense of who I was and how I felt about myself.

The sentence I took the next day to Mrs. A read, "My purpose is to go within and discover the true meaning of chaos and confusion in my life."

Mrs. A smiled at me with a gleam in her eyes and a proud look on her face that I will never forget.

Then she said, "Take this with you forever, Cindy. Your answers tell me that you are on the right track. Every situation in your life is an opportunity to learn who you are, why you are here, and what your higher purpose is. When chaos and confusion confront you, delve beneath the surface and ask yourself these three questions. Go higher and deeper within to find the answers. The voice of your higher self will come forth with the truth you are looking for, as long as you listen. That is your true purpose in this life."

I had no idea what I could possibly learn from my grandmother's untimely death and my sister's life-threatening blood disease. So, I soldiered on, trying my best to put it all behind me.

Five years had now passed since Debby was diagnosed with Lupus. The doctors had found no cure. Thankfully, the drugs they prescribed kept her alive and held her disease in check. Debby's strength was (and still is) a continual source of inspiration to our family and those who know her.

On the other hand, my grandmother's death continued to haunt me. This was partly due to the fact that every day on my way to school we drove by the spot of Janet's tragic accident. Also, no matter how much time passed, something would happen, or someone would say something to remind me of our family tragedy.

One night in particular was during my senior year while at a friend's party. A group of older guys were drinking together and had heard that my father was the owner of Bandini Fertilizer and the famous TV commercial—a thirty-second spot in which a guy slalom skied down a pile of manure while a voice-over said: "Man dares to go where only cows have been before! Bandini is the word for....Fertilizer."

The ad went viral in L.A. before there was such a concept. People even had bumper stickers that read, "I Skied Mt. Bandini."

I was used to everyone commenting humorously on the ad, but that night there was something strange in the boys' voices as they joked about it. Then one of them looked over at me and said, almost bragging, "Wow, you're related to the Bandini crash! Man, we were there. Your grandmother was messed up. She hit her head on the curb so hard it was decapitated. The whole neighborhood was there."

I was in shock. Thinking it was a bad joke, I asked them repeatedly if this was really what had happened. They kept insisting that it was true. They had even named it "The Bandini Crash."

Janet had been killed at Third and Rimpau streets in Hancock Park. I now had visions of lots of people standing around on Rimpau, staring at my grandmother's body lying in the street without her head.

Suddenly it dawned on me, "Had these guys been involved in the crash?"

One of the drag racers responsible for her death had gotten away. The other one, who had crashed into my grandparent's car, was convicted of involuntary manslaughter. These guys were just too cocky and too boisterous not to have been involved, but there was no way to know and nothing I could say or do.

Deeply disturbed, I went over to my boyfriend and told him what I had just heard. I then asked him to please take me home. Yes, Janet was gone, but I knew it was time to talk about it with my parents.

When I told them what the boys had said to me at the party, my dad gently replied, "Cindy, the crash was very violent, but Janet's head was not decapitated."

For the first time since Janet's death, we actually sat down together and truly discussed it.... something we hadn't done since that first night home from tennis camp. Grateful for this moment, I asked my parents every question there was to ask and shared all that I could share.

Finally talking about my grandmother's death cleared up the distress that had been buried inside me for years. It was unbelievably healing to simply spill all of my pain and sadness out onto the table. It would have been so easy to have kept it all buried inside, eating away at me like a hidden cancer. Talking about Janet's death brought closure; it brought certainty that yes, my grandmother was gone, but my love for her lived on.

That night, when we were finished talking, I went into my room and cried every last tear that was left to shed. Afterwards, I felt healed and comforted by the truth that her love is eternal.

At the end of my senior year, Mrs. A chose me to give a speech at our graduation. I called it "The End and the Beginning." I felt that we, the Senior Class, were ending one chapter of our lives and beginning another. Everything was starting anew.

For me personally, all of the questions I had so innocently and urgently asked during these past five years of heartache and confusion were about to be answered—not by any one person, but by the unfolding events of my daily life.

PART 2
WHO
AM
I?

CHAPTER 4

Prophetic Messages Arrive

It was in Israel the summer of 1972 that the first in a series of profound answers began to appear.

I had arrived in Israel through a series of steps, starting with a year at the United States International University (U.S.I.U.) in San Diego/Pt Loma. This led to a semester abroad at the U.S.I.U. campus in Sussex, England. There I met up with Becky, a friend from San Diego. We had similar goals for the summer, so Becky and I hitchhiked together from England to Israel. She was adventurous, full of laughter and smiles, and always ready to explore new things. We were perfect traveling companions.

My parents had sent me a month-long Eurail pass, thinking I would want to see more of Europe. But I sent it back. With youthful exuberance I had decided to work on a kibbutz in Israel, and nothing was going to change my mind. Kibbutzim are organized communities where agriculture is usually the main source of shared income. They are often similar to small villages with lush grounds, swimming pools, and beautiful banquet halls. I was not Jewish, but I wanted to volunteer on a kibbutz and then travel the countryside.

Spending a summer assigned to a kibbutz by the ocean was a dream planted in me by some friends in England. They had raved about their incredible stay at an oceanside kibbutz, but this was not to be for me.

When Becky and I arrived in Tel Aviv, the head office for kibbutz recruitment told us that we were not assigned to a kibbutz by the ocean. However, we were not to worry because all kibbutzim were equipped with swimming pools. A pool was fine, we thought, somewhat disappointed. At least it was water.

After filling out the various forms, we piled into the back of an Israeli army truck late on a full moon evening with a dozen other people we had never met. I happily sat on the end, where the cold steel gate was a welcome arm rest and the open back provided a panoramic view of the Israeli landscape. I listened to the conversations among the people in the truck while gazing out at miles of sunflower fields, enchanting and iridescent in the moonlight.

We drove for what seemed like hours. Becky eventually fell asleep, resting her head of curly light brown hair, thick as a lion's mane, on my sun-burned shoulder. I sat wide awake, observing the land and the sky, wondering how far away we were going and what this experience would be like.

As dawn broke, we started to climb, ever-so-slowly, up the steep incline of a huge mountain. We passed several army trucks filled with armed soldiers on their way down.

"That's odd," I thought to myself.

We finally reached our destination. The truck trundled along a steep dirt road leading into the kibbutz and stopped in front of a row of old wooden barracks painted light green. Before we could even get out of the truck, our Israeli guide stood up and addressed the group.

"There is some information you must know," he said in a commanding tone with a thick Israeli accent. "Do not stray from the road. Landmines have been planted on the hillsides and soldiers have orders to shoot-to-kill after dark."

His speech jarred us into the reality of life on this particular kibbutz. We were completely taken off-guard, and I strained to listen as closely as I could. Suddenly, kibbutz life seemed to be literally a matter of life and death.

Next, he said, "There's a swimming pool a couple of miles down the mountain. If you want a pool here, you'll have to come back next year."

"Unbelievable," I murmured under my breath, looking at Becky as she shook her head back and forth in disbelief.

This was not the kibbutz life that we had envisioned or been promised. Without any warning, we had been placed on the most northern kibbutz in Israel, directly on the border between Lebanon and Syria. There would be no summer by the sea, or even by the poolside. I felt betrayed and more than a bit scared.

The kibbutz we were assigned to was one of the poorest kibbutzim in all of Israel, surrounded by artillery posts and barbed wire fences. Soldiers equipped with machine guns and telescopes manned the military bases on both sides of the border. From their position in Lebanon and Syria, they could even see the rings on our fingers. We were assigned to a military zone, though in a time of peace.

Still, it was a shock. Fighting panic, I went for a short walk on a deserted mountain road that surrounded the perimeter of the property. Knowing from our Israeli guide that the hills were alive with landmines, I made sure not to step off the road.

The main thought running through my mind was, "I've got to get out of here!"

I sat down at the edge of the road and despairingly hurled rocks through the barbed wire fence that defined our kibbutz border. Then I noticed a large, unidentifiable, black animal sprawled dead on the hillside next to me. That was it. I ran back to the barracks, determined to ask for an immediate transfer out of this hellish place.

At that moment of despair, however, fate stepped in.

A group of English students entered our barracks. They had lived for some time on the kibbutz and came to greet us. Happy, jubilant, and full of cheery English felicitations and warm welcomes, they assured us that this was truly a time of peace. The soldiers were not engaged in combat, and they were actually their friends.

The choice now seemed either to follow my heart for adventure or succumb to my fear. Without much deliberation, my heart won out—I decided to stay. Satisfied with my choice, I went to sleep excited to begin my work on the kibbutz pruning grapefruit trees.

I loved my job. Every morning at 6 a.m., we would pile into the large army trucks and hurtle down the mountain to the orchards in the Golan Heights valley. There we were dropped off in front of rows and rows of grapefruit trees, thick with overgrown branches. We were given a pair of pruning shears and left to begin our work.

I crawled underneath each tree on my hands and knees and pruned until I was eventually able to stand up. This process continued until we broke for breakfast at 8 a.m. We then worked with one morning break until 12:30 p.m., by which time it was over 100 degrees and too hot to work. We were back at the kibbutz by early afternoon, ate dinner at 5:30 p.m., and were in bed by 8:30 p.m. to rest up for the next day's work.

I spent each day after work, sitting on the same rock, embroidering, or writing letters to my family and friends. Somewhat compensating for the lack of ocean or pool was a spectacular view of the distant golden mountains of Lebanon and Syria. Painted against a backdrop of crystal-blue sky for endless miles in either direction, the ancient magnificence of the Upper Galilee and the Valley of Dan was astounding. It spread out far below us and served as a breathtaking but subtle reminder that yes indeed, I was on vacation.

It didn't take long until I became close friends with a girl from England named Denise. I nicknamed her Alice because she was magical like Alice from *Alice in Wonderland*. She had short blond hair with rosy cheeks, a buddha-like smile, and shimmering white teeth. Her demeanor was always relaxed and her outlook on life was very spiritual.

Alice had just returned from India and Nepal, where she studied yoga and meditation with master teachers. These transforming practices were completely foreign to me. Luckily, I was inspired by Denise's devotion, and eagerly learned from her the basic principles of Laya (or Kundalini) Yoga. It was a skill that would prove instrumental as events in my life continued to unfold.

I practiced yoga and meditation every day during morning breaks in the grapefruit fields along the irrigation canals of the Golan Heights. What first began out of a need to find some kind of peace in this desolate environment, soon became a spiritual quest. As my meditative curiosity evolved into a dedicated routine, I soon discovered that meditation was the doorway to our place of power within. It was a means by which I could open this door at will, rather than having it swung open for me by trauma and tragedy.

I would sit crossed legged in the fields while passionately asking, "Who am I?" "Why am I here?" "What is my higher purpose in this life?"

The more I focused and concentrated my mind, the easier it was for me to access this place of power. It was as if the beacon of a lighthouse appeared in the distance within, and a hidden empire began settling into view. It was a force that could only be described as an inner connection to the vastness of the universe.

Then I wondered, "Does this place of power provide answers to my deep questions as to who we are and why we are here on this earth?"

At the time, I could only venture a guess. But one thing was for certain. I would stay in Israel for a few more months and then travel to India, thinking maybe there I would find my answers. I was forgetting what Mrs. A had taught me—the answers lie within.

We had now been on the kibbutz for a couple of months, and it was the first cool evening since our arrival. Becky fell asleep in her bed under the one window on the far side of our room, but I couldn't sleep.

An ominous feeling had come over me. It surged through my being, keeping me awake and lying restless in my bed. An endless stream of anxious thoughts raced through my mind as I struggled to determine what was wrong, why I felt so uneasy.

For the first time since acclimating to my unusual environment, I was having serious doubts about being on the northernmost kibbutz in all of Israel.

I wanted nothing more than to fall asleep in a warm bed and

wake up in the morning sunshine. But the call of nature forced me to get up and make my way into the night. The bathrooms were located in a separate building from our sleeping quarters, down a narrow dirt path just past the barracks.

Stepping outside of the pale green dilapidated wooden door, my eyes squinted in disbelief.

"What was going on?" I thought to myself.

It was as if I had just stepped onto the set of a Fellini war movie. Red lights, perched on tall steel structures, flashed on and off, staining the night sky in a translucent, blood-like hue. Flares of light exploded in the distant valley below me as I made my way down the trail.

Suddenly, I noticed a swirl of unaccustomed activity around the bomb shelters. It took but a moment to realize that the soldiers had begun practicing military maneuvers after we went to sleep.

Quickly returning to my barrack I continued tossing and turning, unable to fall asleep. My nerves and instincts on edge, I felt again the gnawing dread I had felt in the car driving home from tennis camp before hearing news of Janet's death, and in the car driving home the night my parents told me Debby was going to die.

This time I knew enough to pay closer attention to all that was happening in and around me. Was Israel about to go to war? Was I now in danger of possibly losing my own life?

Even as these thoughts swirled in my mind, I knew there was nothing I could do for now. The more I struggled with my thoughts and fears, the harder it became to go to sleep. So finally, I decided to practice the meditation techniques I had learned, hoping to replace these disturbing thoughts with more powerful positive ones, or at least be able to relax enough to fall asleep.

I began taking four full breaths, exhaling long and slow as I relaxed deep into myself. After a few minutes, my thoughts and fears seemed to dissolve into the vastness of the universe within me. A pervasive feeling of peace and contentment flowed through my body.

Finally, I fell fast asleep.

It was unclear how long I had slept before being suddenly awakened by a loud, distinct voice adamantly calling my name.

"Cindy!" I heard.

I opened my eyes and saw an ethereal form hovering in the air above my bed.

It was Janet!

At first, I could not believe my eyes. There she remained, my deceased grandmother, looking down at me, through me, into my heart and Soul.

Time seemed to stand still as I felt the loving warmth of her radiant presence. It seemed to bathe the room with a shimmering glow. Janet wore a white robe that appeared to be made of countless tiny electrical lights. She was surrounded by brilliant hues for which there are no words—the gold, violet, and rose colors of her luminous energy.

"Was this real?" I momentarily wondered to myself.

Yet, the soft and comforting warmth of her after-death presence told me this was more real than anything I had ever experienced.

As her angelic presence moved closer to me, a chill ran up my spine. Soon it seemed as if a magnetic shawl had been placed around my shoulders, and a strangely beautiful, yet subtle, pressure filled my chest. It was as if Janet was gently hugging me.

Janet's presence was extraordinarily comforting. I was not afraid, for her serenity put me completely at ease. Her unconditional love surrounded me like a mantle of divine protection.

Then Janet spoke to me.

Her voice was soft, almost a flute-like whisper that resonated inside my head. Lovingly, she told me, "Leave Israel and go back to California."

Janet then showed me a hexagonal-shaped ring, and said, "From this ring will come new understandings."

Her last words were the most poignant of all as she softly said, "I have not left you, but I have not gotten over you're leaving me."

Then, as abruptly as Janet arrived, she vanished.

I laid there for a moment, stunned and motionless as darkness quickly returned to fill the space her radiance had illumined.

"Oh, my God. Oh, my God," I blurted quietly out loud, trying to calm down and catch my breath.

My grandmother had appeared to me like an angel, halfway around the world from our home. She had bathed me in an unconditional love; a love that seemed not of this earth, like a magnificent force pulling me into its glory. I lay there, savoring the remnants of her affection, not wanting to leave its heavenly embrace which seemed to linger like the wake of an electrical storm.

As the afterglow began to subside, however, my critical mind returned with a stream of inevitable doubts. I questioned the experience and wondered, "Did this really happen? Was it a dream or was I hallucinating?"

"Or, had Janet truly appeared in a tangible angelic form and actually spoken to me? Did Janet still exist in some other dimension?" I wondered.

I had no idea, no answers to these questions. Yet I could not explain away the power of the experience, nor deny the reality of what I had seen. As I lay enveloped in an awe that bordered on a state of shock, memories of her death flooded through me.

Within a matter of seconds, a powerful realization set in.

My internal farewell embrace with Janet as a 12-year-old the night she died, and the sense of my grandmother hugging me moments ago in my barrack, had imparted identical feelings of peace and unconditional love. Both times an electrical energy had seemed to envelop my body as we merged into each other.

"Had we actually hugged one another...one flesh-and-blood human hugging a spirit seemingly made of energy and light?" I wondered. "Was Janet actually alive in another non-physical form, and could the veil between our worlds open to allow such intimate contact to be made?" Contemplating these notions was almost intoxicating.

It had never occurred to me until now that my grandmother—her Soul—might be alive and conscious in some other world, in a body of light.

Although I had long questioned the nature of the Soul, it had always seemed somewhat abstract. I had never thought of the Soul as a tangible entity, complete unto itself. I had never considered that a departed loved one, who had shed their physical body, might exist in a Soul body of energy or light that would enable them to still appear to us, to guide and help us.

The idea of ghosts had always seemed like a dark or childish fantasy. Janet had felt more like an angel.

Suddenly, it dawned on me. Our Soul could simply be a body of electrical energy that surrounds and co-exists with our physical body and is then set free once the physical body dies.

These ideas, altogether new to me, and altogether extraordinary, were like precious stones dazzling me with their brilliance. They evoked new feelings within me, connecting me to a higher source of wisdom and spiritual understanding than I had ever experienced.

Questions exploded within me, "Was it possible that death of the physical body was not the end of a life, but only a transition into a new form of existence?" "Were we all eternal beings of light inhabiting mortal bodies of flesh?"

"If this were true," I wondered, "could we consciously exercise the higher energetic nature of our Soul while living in a physical body?" "Could we become higher beings while alive on earth, devoted to transforming whatever darkness we encountered within ourselves or in the world around us into light?"

Janet's appearance, and these ideas streaming through me as a result of our encounter, seemed to have irrevocably changed my previous view of reality, of what was possible, of who I was and why I was here.

As I continued to lie awake in bed, marveling at these revelations, it then occurred to me that Janet had told me to leave Israel and return home. I wondered if her words had anything to do with all the unsettled thoughts and fears I had been reluctantly dealing with these past few hours. Had Janet appeared to give me a warning?

A strong urge to return home had gripped me earlier, but my family was so far away. I did not feel the clarity or strength to radically change my current plans based on the words of an apparition, not even Janet's beautiful presence. Completing my work on the kibbutz and traveling to India remained my only goal.

Janet's final words were the most haunting: "I have not left you, but I have not gotten over you're leaving me."

Her words kept playing over and over in my mind. I wondered what she meant. If she was still alive and present as a Soul, then it was true—she had not left us, and indeed, we had left her.

When Janet died, we had believed and behaved as if she was permanently gone. We had, once or twice on her birthday, visited her grave to pay our respects. But she had, I think for all of us, become a distant memory. It was almost as if we had shut down our feelings and moved on.

The idea that Janet might be present in spirit, receptive to our thoughts, feelings, and prayers, had not occurred to anyone, including me.

In our societal framework, leaving the departed behind and moving on in life was the ordinary thing to do. I never thought, for one minute, that my grandmother might still be alive in spirit, or that our lack of awareness might have caused her any sorrow or pain.

As the dawn light crept over Israel and into our barracks, I lay waiting for the 5 a.m. wake-up call that was now drawing near. I made the most of these last few moments while new life-accelerating perspectives continued to emerge within me.

I felt a desire to fulfill Janet's wish—to acknowledge her presence. Drawing upon the instincts I had felt as a 12-year-old, I now held Janet in my mind and visualized giving her a long loving hug, thanking her for being with me.

Once again, the sense of her presence and unconditional love filled my body. It was as if this simple act of visualizing—myself hugging her with deep feeling—had literally connected me to her Soul.

Then mundane reality abruptly intruded. Literally with a bang and a shout, the long-anticipated knock on the door finally arrived. It was accompanied by a hoarse Israeli male voice yelling, "Wake up call!"

In the hot brightness of the afternoon sun that day, the morning's events took on an air of unreality. By evening, the profound experience of Janet's visitation had begun to seem more plausible as a dream. But it haunted me nonetheless, and the questions it had triggered still lingered in my mind.

On the following day, the physical world mysteriously synchronized with the world of spirit. I unexpectedly received a letter from my dad asking me to come home. For the second time in 24 hours, I was being asked to leave Israel. Dad said that U.S.I.U. San Diego had accepted me for the fall semester, and if I came home, he would help me get an apartment and let me use the extra car at his office.

The timing of his letter aimed at getting me out of Israel seemed a confirmation of Janet's visitation. Yet I still found myself stubbornly resisting, determined to fulfill my own long-cherished plans of traveling to India. Unbeknownst to me, the universe was sending a strong message that I was not able to hear.

CHAPTER 5

The Physical vs. Eternal Self

An integral part of volunteering on a kibbutz in Israel was experiencing the history of the land. So, our kibbutz leaders scheduled a trip to the Dead Sea and the legendary mountain, the Masada—an ancient mountain fortress on the edge of the Judean desert.

The Dead Sea is over 1,300 feet below sea level, making it the lowest land-based elevation on earth. It is also eight times saltier than average seawater. While swimming in the Dead Sea, we were so buoyant from the salt that no matter how hard we tried, our legs would not drop down into the water. All we could do was float on the surface while laughing hysterically. I finally had to get out when the stings from the salt in my pruning cuts became unbearable.

After our swimming excursion, we headed for the Masada. It was early evening when we set up camp at the base of the mountain.

Situated on top of a massive rock plateau, similar to a mesa, the Masada rises thousands of feet above the Dead Sea. Built by

48

Judean King Herod the Great as a place of refuge and a winter resort, the Masada was only accessible by steep narrow pathways wide enough for one person.

After the death of King Herod, the Masada was taken over in 66 A.D. by a band of Jewish Zealots who remained there during the Roman conquest of Israel. When Jerusalem fell into Roman hands in 70 A.D., the Masada was the last Jewish holdout.

For the next three years, the Roman's planned their historic conquest of this nearly impenetrable mountain fortress. They built camps around the base, a siege wall, and an assault ramp from the west up over the summit. By 73 A.D., it was clear that the Romans were going to take over Masada and the Jewish Zealots knew the end was near. Rather than surrender or be captured by the Romans, all 960 Zealots, including women and children, took their own lives.

The area remained uninhabited for nearly 13 centuries, until it was excavated in the 1950's and 1960's. In 1966 the site was declared a national park, and a cable car scaling the mountain was built in 1977. The Masada became, and is today, both a tourist attraction and an Israeli national symbol.

Our ascent to this historic spot was scheduled to begin shortly before sunrise; any later and it would be too hot. The year was 1972, so a cable car had not been built yet. Hoping for plenty of rest before our long hike to the top, we climbed into our sleeping bags just after dusk.

Unable to sleep, I lay gazing into the purplish-blue evening sky. Wispy, ghostlike figures seemed to be floating in the air above us. My friends said they felt a cold, eerie feeling. I recalled years ago reading the story of Black Elk, the Sioux Indian medicine man, who had said a circle protects us. So, I got up and made a circle of rocks around our sleeping bags. But the ethereal apparitions did not go away.

Dawn came, and its light seemed to dissipate the unsettling energy of the previous evening. The overpowering mountain, with its calm, majestic beauty, dominated our surroundings. The path to the top was a steep incline, but I was in awesome shape and ready to make the climb.

We began our ascent as the sun rose over the Dead Sea, turning the mountain a brilliant shade of orange that reflected onto the desert for miles around us. Once again, I felt a sense of awe; a feeling of connection with a power much greater than my mere physical self. The air was infused with an overwhelming sense of peace and tranquility.

I climbed in single-file formation without any problem, pacing myself and applying the breathing techniques I had learned. My body was filled with a kind of pervasive ecstasy.

Then, as if a switch had been flipped, I suddenly felt like I was going to faint. Every step became pure torture. The top of the Masada seemed impossibly distant, and it took every ounce of energy and willpower I had to reach it.

By the time I made it to the top, I was barely able to walk. I spent most of my time sitting on the ancient walls of the ruins. I did manage to wander around a little, and I even saw the huge pit where hundreds of Jews had taken their own lives. I felt then that the disturbance of the night before had been related to the horror of these mass deaths so many centuries ago.

I was examined by a group leader and told I had succumbed to altitude sickness. It hit me so hard that I could only make it down the mountain with the assistance of Becky and another friend, Tony.

Once we reached the bottom of the mountain, the kibbutz leaders gave us a much needed few days off. Becky, Tony, and I decided to go to Jerusalem, and we were dropped off at the gates to the ancient city. Still under their assistance, we searched to no avail for a place to sleep. Walking for what seemed like miles in the growing dark, we finally stopped and laid down in what appeared to be a park.

I immediately passed out.

The next morning, we awoke to find ourselves in the middle of a graveyard. We quickly packed up and began searching the city for a private room in a hostel, but every room was booked. Finally, we found a single bed for me in a room with two other girls. By that time, all I wanted to do was sleep.

When Becky and Tony came to visit the next day, I had become delirious. My eyesight was so blurred that they looked like apparitions standing in the doorway. I was scared. I was too sick to be in a foreign country.

My internal sonar system clicked in, giving me clarity just when I needed it.

Janet's message and my dad's letter, both urging me to leave Israel and return home, seemed undeniably right. Now I wanted nothing more than to be with my family. My dream of traveling to India lost all allure. Filled once more with an eerie dread, my guiding instincts were telling me to change directions and return home. There were just too many signs pointing the way.

So finally, I listened and decided to leave. Becky chose to return home with me, and that afternoon she arranged flights to California for us. Oddly, we both felt tremendous relief at the prospect of leaving Israel, a sign that the right choice had been made.

With our flights booked, I immediately began to recover. There were still a few days left before our departure, so Becky and I decided to travel to the north coast of Israel and camp on the beach. It would be our last chance to spend time by the ocean, and Tony decided to go with us.

On the way, we visited a kibbutz where Tony's friends were staying. It was like a small town, and everyone lived in nice quarters, not barracks. There were no signs of war preparation there; no machine gun posts and barbed wire fences. We attended a huge banquet that evening, complete with singing, dancing, and lots of wonderful food.

I knew then that this, indeed, was what common kibbutz life was really like, and what I had hoped for when I had first arrived.

The next morning, we traveled to the coast and set up camp on the shores of the Mediterranean Sea. There was nothing in sight but endless miles of sand dunes and coastal shoreline. We spent the day relaxing in the tide pools and swimming in the sea.

Late the following afternoon, Becky and Tony decided to go for a walk. I remained at the campsite relaxing in the water and daydreaming about my return home. They were gone for hours. As the sun began to set, dusk was approaching, but there was no sign of them. When twilight enveloped me and Beck and Tony were still not back, my concern began to grow.

Soon nervous thoughts filled my mind. As the sky faded into a deep purple and slowly turned black, I tried to conjure up faith that they would return soon. But the darker it got, the deeper I sank into a paranoid stupor.

As a blanket of stars covered the sky, panic set in. I felt completely isolated and unable to reason away my growing terror that some tragedy had befallen Becky and Tony. Then I began to feel that some awful fate was about to befall me. Unable to turn off this negative whirlpool of fearful imaginings, I left the camp to look for them.

I headed in the direction they had taken, fearfully trudging in the moon-lit darkness up the side of a huge dune. My feet sank calf-high in the deep sand. It felt like heavy weights were tied around my legs. When I finally reached the top, I was out of breath and praying that I would see them from my new vantage point.

Surveying the surroundings, my fear only deepened. All that was visible were endless dunes for miles in all directions. I might as well have been on the moon.

Frightened and utterly alone, I momentarily panicked. I began hyperventilating, stumbling around in circles, desperately looking for help that was nowhere to be found.

Finally, I forced myself to calm down. I knew I had to pull myself together and deal with this. I headed back towards our camp, following the moonlight back to the shoreline.

The choice was mine—whether or not to succumb to my fears.

The tide was low, and still fearing the worst for us all, I made myself lie down in the warm shallows of a tide pool near our camp. I closed my eyes and practiced meditation techniques, focusing my mind and relaxing my body. I visualized myself melting into the rocks and saw an invisible white light surrounding my refuge. I felt protected by this impermeable shield, assured that even if someone with bad intentions came looking for me, they would not be able to find me.

As I opened this doorway within, my fears slowly began to dissolve. Suddenly another, more reasonable, voice emerged within broadcasting the positive perspective that we were safe.

As I held onto that thought a feeling of trust began to take over. It was as if a beautiful force had emerged from the source of my being to show me the way. I sensed that this force was my higher, more enlightened self, now in the lead. The chaotic fearful part of me, wreaking havoc only moments ago, was now nowhere to be found.

Deep in this reflective state, images of the Israeli soldiers flashed before me. Having spent time with both male and female members of the army, I knew their astounding dedication to serving their country. Embraced in the oddly mingled visions of soldiers, protection, and peace, I finally dozed off.

Moments later, however, I was abruptly awakened. Becky and Tony had returned to the camp. Not finding me there, they began to worry and called out my name. They looked relieved as I approached from the nearby tide pools. I was relieved to see them as well, and Becky quickly proceeded to tell me about their adventure.

It turns out, they had been visiting with the Israeli soldiers stationed on the other side of the dunes. Yes, it was true. We were safe.

Later, as I settled in to go to sleep, I contemplated the events of my unusual evening. I noticed two contrary forces had been at work: a normal and reactive part of me full of the thoughts and fear-based perspectives of my physical self, or personality; and a calm and powerful part of me full of the thoughts and trust-based perspectives of my higher self.

I saw that at first, my physical self, my personality, had created a state of fear that became my automatic reality. In the latter part of the situation, my higher self, another voice within me, created a beautiful positive experience devoid of fear, which then became my reality of choice.

By quieting my mind in the face of debilitating fear, a more enlightened self was able to emerge. It was an intelligence I identified as that of my eternal self, my Soul.

My Soul thoughts guided me into a positive and higher state of being. This meant that when faced with adversity, the choice is ours. We are a co-creator of our own experience and reality.

Most importantly, this experience brought forth new insights—the distinction between thinking with the physical self and seeing with the eternal self.

The voice of our eternal self, our Soul, is always present as a higher guiding force—when we stop and listen. It is the same intelligence we become after death of our physical body that's within us now. It is the same eternal intelligence from which Janet communicated, and from which all our loved ones communicate when no longer inhabiting a physical body.

With this realization, the answer to the ultimate question, "Who am I?" was becoming more apparent.

We are both a physical self, a personality, and an eternal self, a Soul, more empowered than ever before to choose higher Soul perspectives when dealing with the challenges and adversity of daily life on earth.

CHAPTER 6

A Name for the Nameless

The flight home to America completed my voyage. India would have to wait.

I arrived in Los Angeles without alerting my family—the element of surprise was my specialty. I called Debby upon arrival at LAX and learned that our parents were out for the evening. Excited to see me after seven months abroad, Debby jumped at the chance to pick me up from the airport.

I then enlisted her help to keep my arrival a surprise, and the plan succeeded. I had the immense pleasure of observing the shocked look on my parents' faces when they came home and found me. As they rounded the curve of the gold carpeted stairwell, I was sitting in a chair at the top. It was like a slow-motion movie. Their faces lit up with more surprise and delight than I could ever have hoped for. We hugged and hugged, and it was so wonderful to feel the warmth of their love. I was home again; tan, healthy, and happier than I had ever been in my life.

This space of happiness was abruptly interrupted two weeks later.

On September 5, 1972, I watched as a special news bulletin interrupted our television program. The news anchor gravely announced the deaths of eleven Israeli athletes and coaches, shot by terrorists at the Munich Olympics.

My heart sank and my Soul grieved for the families of all the slain Israeli athletes in what became known as the Munich Massacre. The first athlete to be murdered was a weightlifter by the name of Yossi Romano. As his dormitory was being attacked, Yossi had tried to overpower his well-armed Palestinian captors, known as "Black September," with a kitchen knife. They shot him four times.

Yossi's wife, Ilana Romano, was suddenly widowed at 26-years-old, with three daughters, the youngest only five months old. Most astonishing was the fact that the night before Yossi left for the Olympics, Ilana spoke openly about her premonitions of an attack. Yossi simply laughed, asking her if she was crazy. Was it crazy? Or had Ilana been listening to her Soul voice, following its guiding instincts and intuition?

There was one thing for certain. I felt a deep bond with the Israelis after my stay there, and I knew this event would further escalate preparations for war.

I immediately wrote letters to several friends on the kibbutz, particularly my yoga and meditation teacher, Denise. Simultaneously, I received letters from them and learned that war preparations now completely dominated our kibbutz. The bomb shelters where we had partied were now true survival shelters, and the serene fields where we had meditated and practiced yoga were now training grounds for the Israeli army.

Denise, who had fallen in love with the Israeli farm manager, had married him in my absence. She described her wedding as a sacred ceremony performed under a cloud of violence. She wrote that life on the mountain was now filled with tension and war. Love and destruction, life and death, were now intermingled in their lives.

Israel eventually retaliated by bombing ten Palestine Liberation Organization (PLO) bases in Syria and Lebanon. The Israeli Prime Minister also authorized the covert operation known as "Operation Wrath of God" to assassinate individuals involved in the Munich massacre. It continued for many years. I never heard from Denise again. In her last letter she wrote, "I shall die confused, but at least I tried to understand."

Residing in the comfort of my home, I acutely felt the power of Denise's conviction. I still think of her often and wonder where she is and if she survived. Relieved to be home and safe, I sat on the side patio of our house and reflected on the turn of events in the last few months.

Once again, the words of my grandmother, "Leave Israel and return to California," pierced my mind.

Janet had come to warn me of the impending violence and possibly save my life. Not only could she see me, but she also had access to these future events and wanted to help me!

The ominous premonitions I had felt that night in my barracks came from deep within me. They were an internal sonar warning me of dire changes, telling me to take notice and prepare. Janet's visitation and my dad's letter had confirmed these deep instincts; signs and messages still denied by my personality. With the onset of altitude sickness, I had been given three messages to return home.

Finally, I had taken action, and for that I felt grateful.

As birds chirped in the trees above me, I contemplated my

remarkable experiences with a surge of unbridled energy. I felt hidden in them, like secret keys, confirmations of the Soul as a living intelligent force beyond the death of the body. They helped to resolve questions I had about the finality of death, and the possibility of eternal life as a Soul, and to the idea that not only can departed loved ones assist and guide us here on earth, but also, we have that same eternal Soul essence within us now, here in a physical body.

I knew that it was time to connect with this eternal force within more intimately.

With the sun now setting in the western sky just beyond the patio vista, answers regarding the hexagonal ring Janet had shown me, and the "new understandings" she said it would bring, still remained a mystery.

However, the place of power within was no longer nameless— it is the home of our Soul!

CHAPTER 7

Voice of the Soul

What had transpired in Israel and the weeks after returning to California was extraordinary. Back home, feeling fragile and a little disoriented, my vulnerability was intensified by one constant concern—was it possible to talk openly about these events without seeming crazy?

My family and friends had heard the mysterious story of Janet's presence and her prophetic warning message linked to the Munich Olympics, but there was so much more to it than that. A magnificent realm, both internal and external to us, had clearly revealed itself.

Yet the events that summer of 1972 had left me living each day feeling like a stranger in a strange land.

Janet's appearance and the insights it triggered were a double-edged sword. On the one hand, they were spiritually enlightening. On the other hand, their very essence challenged the conventional worldview. When I managed to conjure up the courage to talk about my experiences, I was often greeted with understandable skepticism from both family and friends.

I felt as if I were on a tiny boat adrift on an open sea whose vast beauty also contained the potential perils of storms and grueling isolation. From time to time, I felt the comforting presence and mysterious depth of my own Soul, but more frequently, I was battered by the stormy fears, doubts, and loneliness of my personality. At times it threatened to plunge me into an all-consuming sea of negativity, darkness, and despair.

What do we do when our human life is ruled by overwhelming doubts that cover our inspirations with negativity and uncertainty? I had tapped into an extraordinary world during my time abroad. I had experienced unexplainable life-changing events. Now, back at home, alone and unsure, I wanted nothing more than to believe and feel strength and courage. Instead, doubts and skepticism of my experiences still hounded me like wolves howling in the night.

Somehow, I knew I had to face and embrace my fears. I had to accept and love myself as I was, in order to discover and live as what I now knew to be my eternal Soul. But how?

I desperately needed to talk to someone, and finally the opportune moment arrived.

Late that August, our family went on our annual summer vacation to Newport Beach, California. After breakfast one exceptionally beautiful morning, Dad and I went for a walk down to the beach at the Balboa Bay Club.

Standing about 6'1", Dad's curly brown hair blew about in the breeze. He was tanned from the summer sun, making it appear as if his freckles were growing together—a trait he certainly inherited from Janet. Although he was not one to show spontaneous affection, it was obvious by the sincerity in his hazel brown eyes that my dad was excited to be spending quality time with me.

As we passed by rows of pleasure boats rhythmically tapping against the creaking docks, I felt grateful to be spending time with Dad. A flood of childhood memories silently poured through me. I thought for a moment about the times he would play music for us when we were kids. He would sit Debby and me down in two black leather chairs in his den, tell us to shut our eyes, and have us listen to the classical music reverberating through his room.

I also remembered the little wooden box of wise sayings he kept in his desk, and how he'd recite appropriate ones to us from memory when the time was right. They always made us think, and sometimes caused us to laugh. No matter what we were doing in our lives, Dad constantly inquired of us, "What's your goal? Do you have a goal set in your mind of what you want to do in your life?"

As memories settled, I took a deep breath that, upon exhale, sent contentment rushing from my head clear down to my toes. The heat from the sun-drenched pavement warmed the soles of my sandals. The summer air was crisp and clear. The flags adorning the entrance to the docks blew gently in the breeze. The silver clips attached to their hoisting ropes clanged against the tall white flag poles, a sound that will forever remind me of my childhood summers. It was a moment that memories are made of, and I felt serenely happy.

Then a deep uncertainty welled up within me. "Could I tell Dad the intimate details of my Israel experiences?" I wondered.

I had told my family that Janet appeared and said to leave Israel, but we had never sat down and talked about it at any great length. I desperately longed to share with my dad the details and the essence of the Soul insights that had been revealed to me. Yet the urge to hold back was equally as strong. A fear dominated and trapped me: "Will he think I'm crazy?"

As I struggled with the restrictive thoughts that held me back, I felt a deep awareness within me, like a subtle distant voice, saying, "It's okay to be afraid. It's only natural to not want your dad to think that you are crazy or to doubt you in any way. So, go ahead and just be honest. No one can fault you."

Something shifted. I knew in my heart that my fears were okay; they were part of who I was at this moment. And I embraced them. With that, a door to my heart flung open, and the first river of thoughts, feelings, and experiences that longed to be shared came rushing forth.

"Dad, can you believe it?" I asked breathlessly as we continued walking side by side. "Janet appeared to me, told me to leave Israel, and shortly after the Israelis were shot in Munich and war came to our kibbutz? Her Soul must still be alive, able to know the future, watching out for us, and able to communicate with us at times."

The flood had begun, and we both marveled in silence at this astonishing idea.

After a pause, I said, "Dad, my life has been turned upside down since traveling to Israel. What happened that morning was so strange, but it was so real. It made me think that there must be some part of her, a Soul, that's still alive and can still communicate in some form uncommon to us. But there's no one I can talk to about it, and I'm feeling so isolated. I want to confide in you and see if getting it all off my chest would help. There has to be a way to free myself from the doubt and fear I'm feeling, so it no longer consumes me."

As we arrived at the beach and picked up our beach chairs

from the lifeguard station, Dad paused a moment and responded, "Sure, give it a go!"

I mentioned Janet's message, "I have not left you, but I have not gotten over you're leaving me."

"Dad," I said, "if Janet passed away without warning, maybe she also grieved the loss of us?"

Dad looked at me with a gentle smile and answered, calling me by my nickname, "Well, I don't know, Lu."

We found a vacant spot on the beach and spread out our towels on the warm sand. Dad and I settled in for the afternoon as seagulls called out in the distance. I reached for my suntan lotion and began drenching my body in oil as I continued.

"It probably was difficult for her," I exclaimed. "None of us ever considered how it might feel to suddenly find yourself in another reality, without a physical body, separated from your loved ones, able to see them but unable to be seen by them or communicate with them. She was probably with us for a time. But we didn't know she was there."

Our conversation explored the most unusual perspective on Janet's death that had ever entered our minds. "I saw her, Dad, and she communicated with me," I continued. "Her messages were so real. They've left me confused and alone in some way, yet on another level, really inspired."

Dad listened intently, without judgment, as I described Janet's presence in my kibbutz room, and the healing sensations of closing my eyes and hugging my grandmother—and feeling that she, too, was hugging me.

As I shared these profound experiences, a subtle shift continued to occur within me. I felt more and more how beautiful the experience had been for me, and it began to matter less and less what people thought. It was as if the truth of my experience was finally beginning to overpower the demons of doubt and fear.

So, I continued. "Even as a kid, when you first told us that Janet died, I desperately wanted to say goodbye to her. That night as I was lying in bed, I closed my eyes, and with complete trust and a child-like innocence, I saw her in my mind and hugged her with all my might. I felt so much better after our embrace. It was as if a magnificent power had been activated within me simply by visualizing."

As I spoke, I felt a steady stream of evolving confidence. "Dad, it's like there was a wise voice within signaling me all along to leave Israel. But the dominant voice within me—I call it my personality—was determined to stay in Israel and then go on to India. It drowned out the voice of my Soul that knew what was best for me, but I didn't know how to listen. I was determined to stay. Then Janet appeared, you sent me that letter, and I got sick. All perfectly orchestrated to get me to go within and listen at a deeper level."

"Granted," I continued, "it took getting sick for me to finally listen, but when I did, I recognized all the unmistakable signs. I heard the clear and simple message, 'Go home!'"

Dad's expression was thoughtful as he wiped the sand from his bright red swimming trunks, continuing to give me his undivided attention.

"If Janet's Soul still exists in an eternal form," I continued, "then our Souls, our eternal selves, will also continue to exist after our bodies pass away. That also means, they are alive within us right now. I experienced this. I was alone and panicked in the desert, and an inner voice rose up through my fears and provided me with the necessary coping mechanisms. It was a power within, a sense beyond our ordinary five senses. It was the voice of my Soul."

"Dad," I said, "my Soul is helping me talk to you right now, helping me feel confident talking about my experience rather than retreating into my self-doubt."

I stopped for a moment, trying to slow down my racing thoughts just enough to ask, "Does all of this make any sense?"

Dad's reddish sun-soaked face turned abruptly towards me as he replied, "It's all very possible Lu. This will all resolve itself in time for you. You need to decide what you want for yourself right now, what your goals are, and work toward them. Trust me, then everything will fall into place—okay?"

He was right. It was time to move on. But my intuition had been right, and my intentions had worked. The more I shared and explained everything to Dad, the easier it was to accept and assimilate these extraordinary events and embrace who I was now. What a wonderful gift. My dad, by listening with an open mind and heart, gave me just what I needed to move forward in my life.

As we sat in comfortable sunbaked silence, my doubt and fears began to not only dissolve, but to be transformed into trust, a characteristic of my Soul.

It was okay to be afraid. Fear didn't hurt me or imprison me in my personality's limitations if I tuned into my higher self and acted on its deeper impulses. More importantly, I saw that if I viewed and accepted myself from my Soul's perspective, I could begin to bring inhibiting thoughts and emotions into alignment with inspirational feelings.

The secret was to learn to listen to that wise voice within and find peace rather than blindly following my personality into ignorant suffering. This, it now seemed, may be why I am here.

Reclining back on my beach chair, I closed my eyes and entered a state of deep reflection. I saw clearly that it was up to me to accept myself no matter what. When I accepted and embraced my most difficult feelings—fear, insecurity, sadness, anger—they became fuel for my own growth.

In essence, *all* my feelings, experiences, and reactions are essential opportunities to increase my Soul's dominion over my life here on earth.

I saw that when we accept and embrace any situation—and this includes our feelings and emotions—it frees us up to access the higher meaning and energy all challenging moments contain. No one can do this for us or prevent us from doing it for ourselves. It is our essential spiritual responsibility in life.

Yet there was still one more topic I needed to discuss. "Dad," I blurted, "What about Janet's other message? She showed me a hexagonal-shaped ring...I drew it in my journal. She said that from it would come new understandings. What new understandings?"

Dad simply shook his head. He didn't know, and why should he?

Now it was time to put my experiences safely away inside. Dad had lovingly listened, and that was enough for the time being. I felt relief from the overwhelming loneliness of not being able to discuss my experiences. It was scary to be so open, but the rewards were great.

For the first time since returning from Israel, I saw that I might be able to exercise the voice of my Soul and utilize my fears rather than run from them.

Anxious to get up and move around, I looked over at Dad, my eyes squinting from the bright sun and said, "Hey, let's go for a swim."

He was ready to cool off, so we walked together down to the bay. Happy and thankful for Dad's openness and our heartfelt conversations, I reached over and gave him a big bear hug. He too was in an open mood and responded immediately as we simultaneously said to one another, "I love you!"

Our conversations provided a much-needed healing; however, the hexagonal ring Janet had shown me, and the "new understandings" she said it would bring, continued to remain an unsolved mystery.

CHAPTER 8

Fear as Opportunity

O ur summer vacation in Newport was wonderful, yet it flew by faster than anyone would have liked. Soon we were back at home in L.A., and Debby was now getting ready to go away to college for the first time. I was planning to drive her up north to Sonoma State University and afterwards drive back to college at U.S.I.U. San Diego/Pt Loma.

Then news came that my grandfather, Honey, was sick. Even though his actual name was Byron, when Debby and I were kids we heard Janet say things to him like, "Honey could you please pass me the gravy," so, we started calling him Honey. The name stuck!"

Honey still lived in the beautiful home he and Janet had built on Rimpau Ave., overlooking the seventh hole of the Wilshire Country Club golf course. He had remarried a close friend named Betts who we all loved very much, and we were grateful that Honey was not alone.

Late one afternoon while Debby was at a doctor's appointment, I went to pay Honey a visit. As I grew older and had moved away to college, our relationship became more distant, though by no means unloving. Our connections consisted mostly of brief phone conversations. I hadn't been to the Rimpau house in years, and I certainly hadn't seen Honey since Janet had appeared to me in Israel.

As I walked up the brick pathway, the two black stone greyhounds flanking the entrance to the 19-foot white panel front door were there to greet me. Excited at the prospect of seeing my grandfather, yet somewhat timid, I had only one thought as I rang the doorbell, "How sick will he be?"

When Honey opened the tall front, door, I felt like a small child as I reached out to hug him. His blue plaid flannel bathrobe was soft to my touch and his curly, silver-gray hair glistened in the sunlight. He looked thin and pale, yet not as ill as I had feared. The loving smile on his face when he saw me was all that mattered.

As I walked through the familiar marble entryway, I felt a shiver. I had spent so many hours there as a kid, swimming in the pool, playing Perquackey, and cooking with Janet. It suddenly occurred to me that most of my visits in that house were with Janet. I had never really spent much time alone with Honey.

Immediately I wondered, "What will we talk about, and should I mention Janet's visit in Israel?"

We were both happy to see each other. Betts had gone to an appointment, so the two of us strolled through the house as wonderful conversation ensued. Not having been there in so long, I wanted to see every room that I had known so well as a young girl growing up. Honey was interested in my travels, and as we walked along, I told him short tales about my seven months abroad.

When we entered the living room, Honey paused for a moment next to a painted portrait of Janet hanging on the wall above the white linen couch. Then, for the first time ever, Honey opened up to me. He began sharing fascinating stories from his own travels to Europe, which had had a profound influence on his life.

Honey then turned and unexpectedly asked how I was doing. It was as if he knew there was a struggle going on within me. Still hesitant to tell him my story about Janet, I simply discussed with him how I felt a bit of culture shock being back at home.

As we continued to stroll through the house, I could tell Honey needed to rest. He slowly walked over and sat down on an antique stained wooden chair that leaned against the pale- yellow walls of the master bedroom.

Then he gave me a gentle, yet penetrating look, and said, "I can see that you've gained a lot from your experiences and that you'll benefit from them for years to come."

His blue eyes gleamed with the fire of a medieval wizard, and he spoke words which I will never forget: "Embrace who you are now. Have faith in what you believe. And never be afraid to talk about it. Always believe in and trust yourself."

This was the perfect moment to mention Janet's appearance and the effect it had on my life. Yet I didn't want to break our newly formed bond, and I certainly didn't want Honey to think of me as crazy. So, I decided not to bring up my experiences with Janet.

Yet, a seed had been planted with his words of wisdom.

Our short visit lasted nearly an hour. When it was time to leave, I wished Honey a speedy recovery and we shared a powerful hug. A deep happiness emanated from my grandfather, and the broad smile on his face told me we had both been enriched by our visit.

The three-block ride back to my house was serene. All the way I savored a feeling of deep gratitude for Honey's guidance, and for the enjoyable time we had shared.

As I pulled into the driveway of our family home, frustration quickly settled into the pit of my stomach—I had held back out of fear. I hadn't told Honey about Janet's presence in Israel!

Even after my breakthrough talk with my dad, and having acquired many new insights, I felt hesitant. Why, after all this, did self-doubt and the fear of seeming crazy continue to keep me from sharing my most important experiences with the most important people in my life?

I got out of the car and started up the brick pathway leading through the manicured emerald-green lawn. As I reached our front door, a sudden flood of feelings, memories, and insights erupted from the deepest, darkest place within me.

There I was, under the archway where years ago my parents had told me Debby was going to die.

Memories came flooding in, so instead of going inside the house, I sat down on the short brick wall framing our front yard. I recalled the impact of hearing this devastating news which came on the heels of Janet's tragic death. Waves of emotion and insight surged through me.

I reflected on Debby's traumatic illness during our teenage years, and how because I was so healthy, things had seemed good for me at the time. No one told me what to do. I could come and go as I pleased. My life had been fine—or so I thought.

As I adjusted myself on the hard cold bricks, it suddenly struck me that in the commotion of Debby's all-consuming illness, my life as a young girl had faded into the background.

No one ever asked me how I was doing. No one had seemed to realize that I was grappling with my own difficulties. No one had been there to help me with schoolwork or attend any of my basketball games or tennis matches.

Looking back at my life, I saw how in a very real sense I had been abandoned. All my emotions around this had been absorbed at the time by Debby's trauma. They had been buried so deep inside of me for so long I hadn't even known they were there... until now.

For the first time in my life, I felt the heart wrenching pain of abandonment rise from the core of my being.

"Oh, my God," I said out loud.

With that, I burst out crying. Deep sobs welled up in me in waves. "Why did this have to happen?" I thought, as the despair bottled up in me so long ago coursed through me.

I had been carrying this baggage for years and never even knew it. Was this what lay behind my fears of seeming crazy—the fear of being abandoned again?

I didn't know what to do. I wasn't up to talking about this with family just yet. Who knew how they would react? I still had that lurking fear of rejection.

Then, I remembered the insights from my afternoon at the beach with Dad, and Honey's words of wisdom, that I had to accept and embrace the emotions flooding into my being.

I reminded myself that these feelings are okay, they are a part of who I am now. If they remain buried, rejected, or denied, they remain active within me as negative forces, influencing and controlling me beneath my conscious awareness.

It was time for me personally to accept the hand life had dealt me. It was time to put all my fears on the table and see them as the opportunities that they truly are—the chance to grow through life rather than simply go through life.

Once again, the thought ran through my mind, "This is why I am here—to use my fear as the ultimate opportunity."

Satisfied for the time being with having embraced my feeling of abandonment, thoughts then quickly shifted to our impending road trip as I got up and went into the house.

Debby was still not back from the doctor's office, so I grabbed something to eat and reveled in my excitement to drive up the coast and drop her off at the dorm. I had only been to Northern California once on a family vacation and was looking forward to meeting Debby's roommates and spending time with her on this journey. As my dad had suggested in his letter to me in Israel, I had re-enrolled in college in San Diego for my junior year and was excited to reconnect with my friends there.

Waiting for Debby to return from the doctors seemed like an eternity. Still under constant doctor's supervision, Debby was required to take a battery of blood tests to confirm that her Lupus was under control with the drugs, and to get the final thumbs up from the doctors to move to Northern California. We were all packed and ready to go.

"But where was Debby?" "This visit was taking way too long," I worried.

I began to pace back and forth in the kitchen, eager to have her return.

Then by surprise Debby suddenly appeared through the small side entrance in the laundry room used mostly by our pet poodle, Samantha. "What was she doing?" I immediately thought to myself.

Then I saw the distraught look on her face and my heart sank. She shut the door behind her and quickly told me, "The doctors won't let me go."

"No," I cried out feeling like I was living a nightmare. "What happened?"

Debby explained that her blood tests revealed an elevated Sed Rate, and she had to stay home to undergo further medical treatment. I was devastated as my eyes welled up with tears. It just wasn't fair. Not now, not after she had been through so much already and was looking so forward to going to college.

The seven years of illness and uncertainty made Debby strong—stronger than any of us. So, with her usual dignity and grace, Debby began consoling me. Right there in the kitchen, she told me not to worry, that she would be able to go the following semester.

Then the look on her face changed abruptly from one of consolation to concern. The hardest task of all was before her—telling our parents and feeling their pain.

Mom and Dad were upstairs, and I watched as Debby proceeded to do what she had had to do so many times before—deliver more bad news. My parents took the news as best as possible, and we all slipped into what had become our normal response over the years—grieve each in our own way and then try to be strong for Debby.

Always ready to find a solution rather than dwell on the problem, Debby decided to attend USC for her first semester. This meant she could still begin college while living at home and treating her Lupus.

For me, I looked at Debby's bad news as another means to use my challenging fear as an opportunity. It was an opportunity to live in trust—trust that everything would work out for the best.

The next day, I embarked on the two-hour trip back to San Diego. Ready to face whatever new challenges were to come my way, it wasn't long before my life at the very tip of Southern California would be marked by yet another extraordinary event.

CHAPTER 9

A Chance to Practice

The first few months back at U.S.I.U. San Diego had been graced with the immense pleasure of studying with a remarkable English professor, Ken Richardson.

Ken's classes were almost more philosophy than English. While expounding upon literature, he had an uncanny ability to invoke its deeper, hidden meanings. Reaching beyond a story to its essence, he transformed words on the page into wisdom that lit up the minds of his students.

In class, we discussed everything from traditional classics to contemporary spiritual work. Never had I been so educationally inspired and so philosophically ignited.

Ken's passionate personal search for truth added fuel to my own. Many of Ken's students were drawn to him as I was. We frequently went to visit him at the Lodge, a beautiful, historic, Grecian-style building on the Sunset Cliffs in Point Loma, California. The property belonged to the college, and Ken was the caretaker, along with a few of his students.

The entire U.S.I.U. property is rich with history. It was

purchased in 1897 by Madame Katherine Tingley, who was the leader of the American Section of the Theosophical Society. As a member-based organization, it was dedicated to promoting brotherhood and the study of spiritual self-transformation.

Madame Tingley moved the Theosophical Society from New York City to Point Loma—to this beautiful piece of property above the Pacific Ocean she had said came to her in a dream. The community was called Lomaland and housed her Raja Yoga Academy. In 1901, she built the first open-air Greek Theater on the property, where her students performed many classical music concerts and Shakespearean dramas until well after her death in 1929.

In the early 1940s, the Society moved its base to Los Angeles, and the buildings fell into disrepair. In 1952, the property was restored and became the California Western University (Cal Western), and in 1968 was renamed to U.S.I.U. San Diego/Point Loma. It is now home to Point Loma Nazarene University.

The Greek Theatre Madame Tingley built still stands today. During my time on the campus, it became a perfect venue for the U.S.I.U.-sponsored rock concerts we often attended, including Chuck Barry and Linda Ronstadt.

The Lodge where Ken lived was also built by Madame Tingley and was spectacular. The expansive living room where we often met was 60 feet long, with banana trees planted at both ends. A wooden swing hung from the rafters by a large rope, and underneath the swing, brick steps led down to a large sitting area that ran the length of the room. A 20-foot-wide fireplace dominated the far side of the wall and sliding doors on either side opened onto the terrace overlooking the Pacific coastline.

From the terrace, steep stairs descended to a semicircular

landing that led to a path running down through the cliffs toward the beach. At the bottom of the path was a platform carved from the cliffs with the ruins of Grecian-style pillars embedded in the earth. Here it is said that Madame Tingley and her theosophy students held spiritual ceremonies.

Walking up the path from the ocean to the Lodge, white plaster casts of 12 female faces could be seen on the outside of the fireplace wall. They looked like spirits presiding over the house and the sea. These same faces appeared on both sides of the gates entering the driveway and seemed to sustain the mystical aura of Madame Tingley.

We spent many enjoyable evenings sitting in the comfortable chairs on the terrace overlooking the Pacific coastline, sharing, philosophizing, and having wonderful times. Ken, while our professor and very scholarly, also had a knack for being just one of us. These Lodge events often went late into the balmy evenings, and it wasn't unusual for us to simply fall asleep in one of the empty rooms on the property.

Late one such evening, after everyone had gone to sleep, the veil between the worlds unexpectedly parted once again.

I was sitting alone in the den in a mustard-colored velvet swivel chair, listening to the end of a song, preparing to go to sleep. Suddenly, a faint motion in the air near the wooden swing caught my attention. As I watched, fascinated, wispy trails of white light formed in the air above it.

I focused intently and suddenly, to my astonishment, my grandfather, Honey, appeared on the swing.

He looked angelic. His face had the same happy smile as when we last said goodbye just a few months ago at the Rimpau house. But what was he doing here?

I wanted to reach out to him, to touch him and hold him, but my body was completely paralyzed. As I stared at Honey, my body sank deep into the soft velvety cushion of my chair.

Then he spoke to me, though not aloud. I heard his words clearly in my head. "I am going to a good place where you, too, can go," he said softly. "I am happy. Let everyone know.... I am incredibly happy."

With the music still playing, the rapid pounding of my heart and my panoramic view of the Lodge assured me that I was not asleep, that this was not a dream. As I watched transfixed in awe, Honey slowly disappeared, along with the silky glow that surrounded him.

My first thought was to wake someone up, but who? It was too late to call my parents, so I sat glued to the chair, feeling a magnetic field of peace and joy that Honey had left in his wake.

"What had just happened?" I wondered. "Was it real? Honey was still alive. Why would he tell me he was going to a good place?"

Then it dawned on me...perhaps Honey had passed on and had come to tell me?

I got up, wandered down to an extra guest room below the main lodge and attempted to fall asleep to the sound of the waves crashing against the cliffs. But my thoughts kept me awake until dawn.

That morning, I returned to my house to pick up some money. Still feeling disoriented from the night before, I was on my way out when the phone rang. It was my mom. Her voice on the other end of the line was very somber.

"Cindy," she said, "I have some sad news to tell you."

I knew immediately. Oddly, Honey's words from our last

conversation flashed through my mind, "Have faith in what you believe."

"I know, Mom," I said. "Honey passed away."

There was a moment of silence on the other end. "How did you know that?" Mom finally asked.

"He came to me last night and told me," I said calmly, using this chance to practice transforming my fear of seeming crazy.

Mom had received many spiritually searching letters from me in Israel and had heard my Soul stories. But this incident added a new dimension of reality to my testimony of other-worldly experiences. I didn't say anything more about Honey's appearance. I told Mom that I loved her and said I would make plans to fly home immediately.

Honey had asked me to let everyone know that he was happy. Yet, I didn't know how I was going to do this. I wasn't about to make a public announcement to everyone. But I knew I had to find a way to fulfill his last request.

A few weeks later, Honey's funeral day arrived. Our family and a group of Honey's closest friends were gathered in the living room of the Rimpau house waiting for the funeral limousines to arrive. Our whole family gathered around Honey's wife, Betts, knowing how hard his death was for her to bear.

When Betts left the room, I instinctively followed her, feeling an urgent need to relay Honey's message. I also felt nervous and reluctant to speak to her. But the insights and experiences of the past several months now informed my awareness.

Once again, I knew that, even in the most challenging situations, I could use my fear as an opportunity to free myself up for higher guidance to come through. Here was another chance to practice. I told myself, my fear was okay. And in knowing so, I consciously embraced and released my fear, silently calling upon the higher power that resided within me. As I did so, I felt my fear dissolving.

At that moment, I glanced outside the kitchen window and saw a rainbow form in the mist hovering above the sprinklers on the lawn. It was pure serendipity.

I grabbed Betts' arm and said, "See that rainbow arched across the water?" At first, she didn't see it, so I pointed it out again. Then her eyes lit up with sudden delight.

"Honey is in a place just as beautiful as that rainbow," I told her with complete assurance. "He's as happy as that rainbow makes you feel. He appeared to me after he passed away the other night and asked me to tell everyone this."

Betts turned to me with tears in her eyes and a huge smile on her face. Then she held me tightly and said, "Thank you, thank you!"

I couldn't help wondering if Honey had a hand in creating this timely rainbow miracle.

As Betts and I returned to the living room, a loving presence seemed to surround me, and I felt a lightness of being as I walked through the house. Looking upward for a moment, the words "Thank you" formed spontaneously on my lips. I knew that I was not alone.

The limousines finally arrived, and the funeral procession started across Los Angeles toward the Forest Lawn chapel in Glendale. Our family arrived first, and we took our seats in the chapel, to the left of the pulpit. I was sitting next to my dad.

Strangely, we were concealed from the other guests by a black curtain that hung just this side of the casket. Feeling isolated, I knew that another challenge lay before me—to relay Honey's message to Dad.

As we sat waiting for the others to arrive, I felt a palpable, eerily familiar magnetic force beside me. I had felt the same energy on the nights that Janet and Honey had appeared to me. Had Honey come to witness his own funeral?

I suddenly recalled Janet's communication that she had not left us, but that after her death, we had left her. So, I immediately turned my attention to Honey. I saw him vividly in my mind and felt his presence. Without hesitating, I embraced him Soul to Soul with total joy and unrestrained emotion.

"I love you," I told him silently.

Honey, too, embraced me. It felt too real to be my imagination.

In the sweet silence, I knew the perfect moment had come. Hesitating slightly, I leaned over and whispered earnestly into my father's ear, "Dad, it feels like Honey is here with us. He doesn't want you to worry. He's happy. He's gone to a good place." Tears welled up in both our eyes. "I know this may sound strange, Dad," I continued, "but believe me, he's really anxious for you to know this."

As the sadness on my father's face began to melt, I knew that on some level he believed.

Then Honey's advice, "Have faith in what you believe," coursed through my mind. I was now experiencing the power of this admonition. Faith held what I saw as real, and faith held me in its arms.

I sat quietly beside my dad as the chapel filled up with mourners. It was now time for the funeral sermon to begin. The preacher was a kind-looking gentleman, perhaps 70-years-old, with white hair and rosy cheeks. His red and white robe flowed gently to the floor, and from our seats we could clearly see every move and gesture he made.

I braced myself for the sermon, expecting him to talk about the sadness of Honey's passing. Instead, he spoke passionately, calling Honey's death not an end to be mourned, but the beginning of a new life, and an occasion for rejoicing.

"So, let's not take pity on this man who lived his life to the fullest and has passed away. Let's rejoice for a man who, having lived this life to the fullest, has now passed on into a new life."

His sermon penetrated deep into my heart. It felt like a confirmation of my recent experiences, and of my changing understanding of life, death, and the mysterious world that lay beyond.

After the funeral, our family led the procession to the mausoleum where my grandfather's casket was to be placed in the wall. We walked down a long marble corridor, with open rooms on either side filled with rows and rows of plaques dedicated to those who lay interred within.

As we approached the space reserved for Honey, the procession came to a halt. Yellow roses draped his casket, and we formed a single line behind it.

As soon as we were all in place, the preacher, without speaking, began moving down the line from person to person, gently and lovingly clasping their hands, paying his respects to each member of our family. I saw each person take comfort in his smile and find consolation in the beams of warmth he conveyed through his eyes and from his heart.

When he reached me, however, his demeanor changed.

The preacher clasped my hand with great intensity and held it tightly between his own, as if in prayer. He then placed my hand on his heart, and with an overwhelming affection, he said, "Blessings to you!"

He paused a moment longer, as if taking comfort in the light that I had felt surrounding me since the funeral began. Then he gave me the sweetest smile, released my hand, and moved on.

Over time, the intensity of the events that had occurred, both in Israel and at home, would fade. Yet the inner shifts catalyzed by these experiences would deepen and become more stable in me as I was continually given a chance to practice the new insights and enlightened perspectives available to us all.

An inner veil had parted to reveal my Soul as a locus of wisdom and spiritual power residing within. I found myself moving forward each day with a new freedom, clarity, and sense of why I am here.

My life now felt like a quest—for growth, for insights, for a chance to practice. I found a simple affirmation to anchor my awareness in the new insights I had acquired: "May I always recognize and embrace the intricacies of my personality, tune into the higher wisdom of my Soul, and always know the difference."

I have learned that life is full of mystery. Nothing can truly be proven, and that is the beauty of the spiritual realm. Many things can be explained away as messages from our subconscious or simply vivid dreams. But there is so much we simply can't yet explain.

So, I kept on with my life, not knowing all the answers and not knowing where to find them. Still feeling isolated and alone with my experiences, my faith that spiritual companionship would come my way did not disappoint.

PART 3
SOUL
DESTINY

CHAPTER 10
Wisdom from India

It was now late fall of 1972. As the extraordinary events of the previous few months began to quiet down, one prevailing question remained—why me?

Living simply as an average junior in college, there was nothing extraordinary about me. I was not trained as a medium, and there was no way to explain my grandmother's appearance seven years after her fatal accident, nor my grandfather's visit at the same moment he passed on. It didn't make any sense.

Somehow, I had to find answers. Someone else must have had similar experiences. Someone else must have learned about the nature of the Soul and the possibility of non-physical beings intervening for purposes of help and guidance in human affairs.

I knew the answers would come when I least expected them. I also knew it was time to move on with my life. Specifically, I had to find a way to manage another reoccurring challenge I faced—a previous breakup with my first love, Christopher.

Prior to travelling abroad, my freshman year at U.S.I.U. San Diego/Point Loma campus had revolved around my relationship with Christopher. He was the campus musician; a sophomore renting his own home and a fun-loving, popular surfer guy.

We spent a great deal of time together, laughing, partying, and visiting family and friends. We never fought and had nothing but the utmost love and respect for one another—until his decision to transfer to the Mexico campus cut our relationship short.

Being an international university, U.S.I.U had campuses all over the world. I had hoped my parents would let me transfer to the Mexico campus as well, but that was not meant to be. They wouldn't agree to pay for my education if I transferred, so Christopher and I were forced to continue on apart.

On the eve of Christopher's departure for Mexico, we went to see the original film version of Pollyanna at the Los Angeles Museum of Modern Art. Our impending separation cast a shadow of sadness around us, but this quickly dissipated as the movie got underway. We both found great solace in Pollyanna's character, especially her famous line, "I'm glad because you're glad!" This phrase became our mantra, and we left the theater happy for one another's new journey.

However, that night our final affectionate goodbye was a haunting omen. We hugged for what seemed like hours, and repeated Pollyanna's line, "I'm glad because you're glad." But as I released my fingers from Christopher's shoulder-length straight blonde hair and reluctantly pulled my arms away from his soft, forest-green corduroy coat, fate had been set in stone.

Through a series of miscommunications and ongoing assumptions, the distance had torn us apart. I dabbled in a new relationship thinking Christopher had met a girlfriend in Mexico, when in fact they were simply friends.

When he returned to San Diego the fall of my sophomore

year, I realized that remnants of our powerful love still resided within me. By that time, however, Christopher had wanted to just be friends.

To make matters worse, Chris and I had both decided to attend our second semester that year at the U.S.I.U. Campus in England. This time my parents supported the decision. For a moment I was excited that this meant we could finally get back together. However, that notion was short-lived when Christopher told me he was excited to travel to England together and made sure that I understood that we would do so as friends.

The news was devastating.

So before flying from L.A. to Heathrow, the need to buy a spiritual book lured me into Pickwick Bookstore on Hollywood Boulevard. There, the miracle happened.

A book suddenly fell off a nearby shelf, and I instinctively went over and picked it up. It was entitled *The Knower and the Known*, by J. Krishnamurti.

I hadn't heard of the author at the time, so I took a moment to read the back cover and the table of contents. Krishnamurti was a philosopher from India, and it quickly became apparent that this book was exactly what I needed to guide me through my painful breakup and my impending journey to England.

Had I actually been guided to this book? My own intention had originally sent me to the bookstore, but it was as if an invisible hand pulled *The Knower and the Known* off the shelf for me to read. This book had become my bible and Krishnamurti became my mentor while finishing my sophomore year in England, unable to be with the one I loved.

Now, back in San Diego for my junior year after seven months abroad, I needed to find help. I *still* wanted to mend my broken relationship with Christopher. Even though he had broken up with his girlfriend at the time, we simply remained good friends and still are to this day.

However, living in the same small town as Christopher was a constant source of agony. I was unable to manage my feelings for him. It was as if news of a death in the family had struck once again. At 20 years old, my life was surrounded by a pervasive sadness.

I wanted nothing more than to live in the moment, to work through my sorrow and control it, rather than having it control me. In more distress than I could manage, I needed more strength than I could conjure up.

My only recourse was to climb out to the edge of the cliffs and beg the ocean for guidance. The cold, hard agony pounding inside forced me once again to reach out to places unseen for help. Crying out and really not knowing who was listening, I threw every bit of my anguish to the waves below me and pleaded for assistance.

Luckily, faith was once again my guiding light. With a renewed sense of dedication, I turned my back to the ocean determined to continue on with my life, knowing that help would come in one form or another.

This time, isolation was not part of the struggle. Certainly, everyone had at one time, or another endured this same relationship pain. My battle was to survive each day without breaking down.

I had hoped meditation would help, but no matter how long or often I meditated, my pain was still there when I awoke each morning. I did not know how to maintain the peace of meditation amidst the frustrations of my daily life. It was one thing to meditate while I was in Israel surrounded by grapefruit trees and the peaceful irrigation canals of the Golan Heights. It was a completely different thing to meditate in the solitude of my room, and then go out into the challenging, fast-paced western world and face seeing Christopher.

For that, I definitely needed more tools.

Then, help appeared through an old friend—*Knower and the Known*.

For the first time since England, I pulled out my book, now ravaged by use. I read it once again cover to cover, this time from a new perspective. Krishnamurti's teaching further validated the insights I had acquired since living in Israel.

His teachings reminded me to observe difficult emotions like sorrow and fear without resistance, just as I would watch the weather—a rainstorm or a cloudy day—without struggling against it or trying to change it. I was learning to accept my pain and difficult feelings as weather patterns in my inner landscape, as a part of me to simply observe. And the more I embraced this awareness, the more the pain of my breakup subsided.

Gradually, my focus changed. I began to concentrate on bringing spiritual solutions into my life. I firmly encouraged myself, "Okay, let's get off this misery-go-round and find a better horse to ride in a positive direction." No one could do this for me. It was time to be my own coach. It was time to mentor myself and transmute this sadness into positive action.

Then welcome news of my acceptance to Sonoma State University came at a perfect time. By January, I'd be moving to Northern California, hoping that Debby would be joining me. I looked forward to living close to my sister and to finally being free from the pain of my breakup with Christopher.

In the meantime, living in the college party scene while trying to meditate and practice yoga three times a day was a challenging task. More often than not, drinking and clubbing won out.

For the fall semester, I had rented a beautiful house in Point Loma with three other friends. It was a simple yellow ranch-style home situated on the upper tier of streets lined off the face of the Sunset Cliffs, giving us a panoramic view of the entire Pacific coastline. We were right down the road from the Pt. Loma Campus and the Lodge where my grandfather had appeared to me.

Every night, the sunset radiated into our living room with beams of orange dancing light, which was a welcome relief from a world in which I no longer seemed to fit. The sun's brilliance as it disappeared between the golden sky and the shimmering blue ocean was warm and comforting, but still failed to alleviate the isolation that continued to envelop my life.

Unsuccessful efforts to meld my social and spiritual life kept me confused and distressed. Even though partying quickly became a priority, meditating was a compelling need. No matter how many times I attempted to engage in metaphysical conversations, they were acknowledged but inevitably dismissed in favor of drinking, dancing, and romancing.

I loved partying with my friends and having conversations with my dad. I was grateful for the preacher's sensitivity at Honey's funeral, but there was still no one to really talk to. I still felt very isolated. I had to figure out a way to blend the extraordinary episodes of the last few months into a world that was cut off from extra-dimensional experience.

I had new insights sitting in the top drawer of my spiritual tool chest. Now it was time to use them.

It was imperative that I continue to infuse my derailing thoughts and emotions with the higher light and insights of my Soul, which I knew to be my deeper, truer self. My Soul's comforting voice whispering within was calling me beyond the unfolding drama of my life, saying, "It is okay. Things will work out."

One evening as I sat watching the sunset from the luxury of my living room, I decided to close my eyes. I practiced focusing on my isolation and all of the emotions it invoked in me, trying to see them without judging, reacting, or wanting to get rid of them—accepting and embracing them as a part of who I was.

Within minutes, their all-consuming hold on me began to dissolve, releasing me from their bondage. As the sun beamed through the window onto the spot where I sat, I knew then things were going to work out. All I needed to do was to hold on to that perspective.

So, I established an evening ritual and closed each day with a fervent prayer for spiritual companionship and the strength to maintain higher perspectives.

As the fall semester of my junior year ended, I was anxious to go to Sonoma State and meet up again with my friends from the U.S.I.U. England campus. We had all become close living in an old English monastery in the middle of the Ashdown Forest in Sussex, England. They were now living on a family ranch on Sonoma Mountain and had invited me to live with them. It was near Sonoma State outside a small town called Petaluma.

"Petaluma?" I had thought to myself. "That's a weird name for a town."

While finishing the fall semester, I continued to enjoy English classes with Ken Richardson, who often spoke about his two sons Dan and Dave.

Some of the memorable tales involved adventures at their home in Priest Lake, Idaho. Dan and Dave built a double-decker treehouse five stories off the ground and then hoisted a wood burning stove up to it on a pulley. Ken also told us how, rather than paying for their college education, he bought Dan and Dave a cabin on a piece of land in Montana which they named Rivendell. "Life would be their education," Ken told us.

Totally intrigued by these stories, I hoped to meet Dan and Dave someday.

That meeting came sooner than expected. One morning I walked the few blocks from my house down to the Lodge for a short visit when Dan arrived with his girlfriend, Terri.

They were an intriguing couple. Terri had long, dark, silky Polynesian-like hair and beautiful green cat-shaped eyes. Dan was serious with the same sage-like quality as his father—his deep-set brown eyes reflected mysterious wisdom.

We introduced ourselves and I immediately asked where they were from. To my astonishment, Terri replied, "We live in Petaluma."

I couldn't believe it! Petaluma? The same strange-sounding town where my friends had invited me to live!

Over the next few days, we easily struck up a friendship and spent many hours sharing stories and getting to know one another. Electricity resonated throughout our conversations, ignited from our discussions on philosophy, metaphysics, eastern religion, and music.

The feeling was indescribable—my prayers had been answered.

When I mentioned my unfulfilled plans to go to India, Terri insisted that I meet Dan's stepbrother Peter Peringer. She described him as a 14-year-old prodigy who played Indian tabla drums. Pete had just returned from a trip to India, where he had studied tabla with the great masters.

"He went to India?" I gasped as a strange sense of eternity seemed to connect us. I knew without a doubt, I had to meet Peter—another link to India had arrived.

The companionship I so longed for was now right in my backyard. An inner knowing raced through me with the speed of light, followed by a wave of gratitude.

This was no coincidence. It was not only an answer to my prayers, but it was also a signal from the powers of the universe that I was on the right track; a minor miracle drawn by my desire for spiritual growth and my yearning for truth.

As awakening moments continued to emerge, it became apparent that when we stop and listen within, we connect with the intelligent mystical powers at work in the universe. Within and all around us, they speak a language of their own, hear our every thought, answer our every prayer, and meet our essential needs. They do so always at the right time and in just the right way, through the events, circumstances, and people in our life.

My job now was to wait patiently for Northern California to become my home. My practice of saying daily prayers out on the cliffs soon evolved from the mere need for companionship into requests for more knowledge about all that had transpired recently. I knew that it was imperative that I take time to go within and coach myself beyond the current challenges of my life—living in the same town with someone I genuinely loved but couldn't be with and melding my spiritual needs into a world where spirituality wasn't a priority.

It seemed, however, that the more answers I was given, the more there was to know.

Soul Destiny

While connecting with one of my roommates, I finally opened up about my struggles. To my surprise, she reciprocated by sharing her own struggles, and then told me about a church known as the Self-Realization Fellowship (SRF). She explained that it was founded by a philosopher and master teacher from India named Paramahansa Yogananda.

Without hesitation I signed up for their weekly home study courses and started attending church services. The Self-Realization Fellowship was in beautiful Encinitas, CA. I had only known this location as the popular surfing spot "Swamis." Now, SRF and its meditation gardens on the bluffs overlooking the Pacific Ocean became my refuge.

Most importantly, my third link to India had now appeared— this time to provide me with the most definitive answers to date.

One day, Ken's younger son, Dave, arrived at the Lodge from Seattle. Dave was sensitive and kind. He had a loving smile and like his father had an open heart. He was staying in a small bungalow tucked away below the main Lodge. The ocean crashed right up against the cliffs that formed the front yard of his room and the picture windows inside provided a panoramic view of the entire coastline.

While in his apartment one afternoon, a familiar piece of paper tucked away under his books caught my attention. I realized it was from the same Self-Realization Fellowship home study courses that I was taking. Dave and I began discussing Yogananda's teachings and even attended church services a few times together.

It was as if the louder I knocked on the door of life, the wider it opened; like floodgates lifting in front of a dam. There was now an abundance of companionship coming my way.

98

Then, finally, the long-sought-after set of answers about the nature of our Soul miraculously appeared.

As I was studying Yogananda's *Autobiography of a Yogi*, radical concepts on telepathy, masters of time and space, the sixth sense, and life beyond death surfaced. Yogananda wrote about the ability of Souls no longer in physical bodies to materialize and dematerialize at will in recognizable form. He wrote about the science of telepathy (thought transference). Yogananda described how thought vibrations in one man's mind, either alive or dead, are transferred through the ethers, creating electrical waves that in turn transfer themselves into thought waves in the mind of the other person.

That was what my grandparents had done!

Honey and Janet had materialized in a physical form and spoken to me telepathically. Yogananda's writings explained and confirmed for me that my encounters with my late grandparents were not simply messages from my subconscious, they were authentic telepathic communications between spirits embodied and disembodied.

Why was I able to see and hear my late grandparents so easily?

To find an answer, I delved deeper into the spiritual science behind the art of yoga and meditation. I discovered that through meditation, the inner eye, our sixth sense or intuition, is opened up. The human mind is thus empowered to see and hear beyond the ordinary five senses we are all familiar with.

I had been meditating three times a day for two months when Janet had appeared in Israel, and I was working to maintain my meditation routine when Honey appeared. This practice must have opened up a receptivity that lies dormant when not exercised.

Typically, as children we are taught to exercise our bodies and our minds, but far too often to ignore our Souls. As infants, we naturally tap into the higher frequencies of the universe. Then through the process of socialization and education, we gradually lose our innate connection to our Soul and are cut off from its intuitive wisdom and inner voice.

Yogananda's words show us that there is a culture in the world that not only acknowledges extrasensory phenomena, but also incorporates it into the very framework of society. Was this the reason I was so drawn to India? I believe it was.

Now I saw that his spiritual science, handed down for millennia by the saints, sages, and philosophers in India, was a bountiful source of wisdom that we can draw upon; that can help us connect with our Soul and live a more enlightened life.

But how can the Soul become more fully incorporated into the world in which we live today? Very often we don't use telepathy, or the Soul, or the sixth sense in our homes or our businesses or our recreation—at least not consciously.

Further answers were to be revealed, but in the meantime, I wrapped up the fall semester of my junior year in San Diego and put all my energy into moving to Northern California. There, unfolding events would soon take me on a radical change of course.

CHAPTER 11
Our Higher Purpose

As Debby had predicted, she was able to attend Sonoma State the winter/spring semester of 1973. She had originally been assigned to live in the dorms, and due to her unusual circumstances, they had held a room for her. Now both of us were moving to northern California, so Mom and Dad drove Debby up with all of her things to help get her settled.

Dan and Terri were leaving for Petaluma the same weekend I had planned to fly to San Francisco, and I accepted an invitation to drive up with them. I was sad to leave Southern California, but it couldn't have come at a better time.

The seven-hour journey seemed like a magic carpet ride. I was moving on to a new life. Eager to hook up with my sister, my friends on Sonoma Mountain, and finally be free of my past, I did not have a care in the world.

Once we reached Petaluma, I stayed at Dan and Terri's house for a few days. I had never been to Sonoma County, nor seen the weeping willow trees and broken-down chicken coops that represented Petaluma, the one-time "Chicken Capital of the World."

Dan and Terri wanted to move into a new house, and the extra money I contributed meant they'd be able to afford a better one. So, I decided not to move to Sonoma Mountain and looked for a place to rent with them.

Until we could find a new place, the living room floor in their two-bedroom house became my sleeping quarters. I frequently went to visit Debby in the dorms and to see my friends from the England campus way at the top of Sonoma Mountain.

With my sister now at college, the years of struggling with her illness had taken its toll on my parents, and they decided to separate. Dad was now living alone and made a few trips up to Northern California to visit us. We enjoyed taking him to the beach at Bodega Bay or up to Sonoma Mountain for a barbeque and a panoramic view of the Northern California countryside. Dad eventually married my godmother, Jeanne, and often they would travel up together to visit us.

Settling into my new life in Northern California, Dan, Terri, and I continued to build a wonderful friendship. Then late one afternoon, Dan decided to pay his stepbrother, Pete, a visit. I was excited to finally meet this person who was so reverently respected, and the anticipation mounted as we approached his house in southern Marin.

We rang the doorbell, but no one was home. Disappointed, but knowing we would call again, I followed Dan and Terri as they peered into the living room window. There was no furniture to be seen, and Indian rugs covered the parquet floors with all sorts of ancient-looking Indian instruments positioned around the room. It felt as if we were looking in on someone's inner sanctuary. I stared through the window for as long as possible, mesmerized by the stream of light focusing like a spotlight on the instruments we were admiring.

A couple of weeks later, Dan, Terri, Debby, and I visited a poet friend of the family, and I will never forget my first introduction to Pete.

He made a grand entrance, whirling into the room with an energy that bounced off the walls, like balls of electrical light. Now 16 years old, Pete was like a wild boy in from the jungle. He had a strong stature and rusty brown hair that rested gently in curls on his shoulders. Peter's face was sculpted, resembling Michelangelo's David, and fire welled up from deep within through his golden-brown eyes. He was wearing a navy-blue collared polo shirt with white pinstripes and blue jeans that rested way below his waist with giant holes in each knee.

Before Peter extended greetings with everyone, he respectfully removed his wooden leather-strapped Indian sandals and placed them carefully by the door. He was excited to see everyone and gave Terri a big kiss. When Terri introduced him to Debby and me, he smiled a genuine yet cautious smile. I had never met someone so full of life. Pete was like a bolt of lightning, and the light from his eyes held deep secrets.

That night, Pete and his tabla drums came to stay with us in Petaluma. In fact, he and I shared the living room floor.

Many nights, all of us stayed up late as Peter played his favorite album, *Drums of North and South India*. He knew every rhythm count and drum syllable on every track. Peter recited each composition with indescribable intensity, particularly the ones he loved most. His knowledge of the music was remarkable for someone so young.

Ignited by Pete's enthusiasm, we listened to each piece of music again and again. He showed everyone the mechanics of the music and taught us how to keep "tal" or count a cycle of 16 beats on our hands. I was completely new to this musical form, and it was an intoxicating experience.

The tabla is a set of two drums covered with goatskin, a baya or round metal bass drum, and a tabla or round wooden treble drum. They are played with the fingers of each hand while the person playing recites compositions that are simultaneously transformed into drum patterns.

When I left for school each morning, Peter started his tabla practice. When I returned at the end of the day, he was still sitting in the same position, practicing, even though he had a deep split in the middle of his index finger.

Pete was consumed with the drums and their intricate rhythm patterns. By the age of 16, he had already traveled to India twice to study and perform with the great masters there, and his musical talent was highly respected by all who knew him.

Peter and I became fast friends. He usually stopped practicing when I arrived home and we talked for hours. Sharing endless stories, we easily related to one another on a deep spiritual level. Pete described his life in India studying with master musicians while I told him about my travels to Israel.

We delved into my experiences with both Janet's and Honey's presences. He was extremely interested because, even at 16-years-old, Peter believed that there was an accessible power beyond physical reality. My stories verified his own beliefs, and we found great companionship in one another.

Peter was on a break from the Ali Akbar College of Music (AACM), a school of classical North Indian music in Marin County just north of San Francisco. Ustad Ali Akbar Khan (Khansahib) ran the school.

Considered a national living treasure in India, Khansahib was admired by both Eastern and Western musicians for his brilliant compositions and his mastery of the sarode—a beautiful, 25-string Indian instrument. Lord Yehudi Menuhin, the great concert violinist, called Ali Akbar Khan, "An absolute genius... the greatest musician in the world," and he is considered by many to be the "Indian Johann Sebastian Bach."

Khansahib first founded the Ali Akbar College of Music (AACM) in Calcutta, India, in 1956. Later, recognizing the growing interest and the extraordinary abilities of his Western students, he began teaching in America in 1965. In 1967, he founded the Ali Akbar College of Music, which moved from Berkeley to Marin County the following year.

Khansahib taught and performed at the College until just before his death in 2009. The AACM has always been, and still is today, a wonderful place to learn the classical music of North India, even on non-Indian instruments such as violin, cello, guitar, or flute.

My first exposure to AACM came in 1973, when I drove Peter from Petaluma to his classes at the college, then located just outside the small town of Fairfax, California.

Pete studied with Ustad Zakir Hussain, the preeminent classical tabla virtuoso of our time and the foremost disciple of his father, the legendary Ustad Allarakha. Zakir was a child prodigy who began his professional career at 12-years-old, accompanying India's greatest classical musicians and dancers and touring internationally with remarkable success by 18-years-old.

Zakir began teaching at AACM in the summer of 1972. He had accompanied Khansahib in concerts at the College prior to that, but it wasn't until after Zakir taught a summer tal class that he became the full-fledged tabla master at the college in the fall of 1972.

Watching Zakir perform at the college and other local venues was, and still is, a magical event.

Zakir is not just a master drummer. He is one of the most brilliant and sensitive musicians I have ever seen. A New York Times article in 2008 described his talent this way; "Tabla master Zakir Hussain, a living genius, whose unadulterated performances of Indian music are among the most thrilling anywhere..."

During his performances, Zakir, together with the instrumentalists, has the unique ability to create a musical journey that's encircled in an unforgettable rhythmic experience. In the almost 50 years I've heard Zakir play, each and every time—without fail—he blows my mind. And metronomes bow before him!

Zakir bridges the gap between entire cultures with his art, tying together improbable threads of connection between musicians of all musical genres. Zakir's brilliant accompaniment, solo performances, and genre-defying collaborations have globally elevated the status of his instrument, bringing the tabla into a new dimension of renown and appreciation.

Zakir is widely considered a chief architect of the contemporary world music movement and in 2017 he was honored with SF Jazz's Lifetime Achievement Award in recognition of his unparalleled contribution to the world of music.

His many historic collaborations and contributions to world music include the two bands, the Diga Rhythm Band and Planet Drum, founded with Mickey Hart, drummer for the Grateful Dead. Zakir also formed the band Shakti with John McLaughlin and performed with George Harrison on his album *Living in the Material World*.

Most recently, Zakir and Mickey Hart have teamed up and created *Sound Consciousness: Drones for Sonic Bathing*, a healing, meditative journey through rhythm and sound.

I was privileged to attend many of Peter's private classes and experience this ancient musical art form through the genius of Zakir Hussain.

Throughout their sessions, the rapport between Pete and Zakir was extraordinary. Zakir recited intricate compositions. Peter heard them once and then recited the syllables as he transferred them into rhythm patterns on the drums. They were so in sync that Zakir knew instinctively what Peter was going to do next—then took him one step further. Peter responded by not missing a beat.

Most astounding was that none of Pete's lesson was written down. The music was simply taught through recitation, as it had been for thousands of years. It was evident that Zakir was very inspired to teach such a talented young boy as Peter.

The most ironic factor in all of this is that I had wanted to go to India less than six months before meeting Peter, but now the music, the people, and the philosophy of India had traveled to me.

While watching Peter master his art, the parallels between Indian music and Soul awareness soon became apparent.

Peter's will and dedication to the tabla exemplified what was required to go within and coach ourselves to achieve inner results. The same effort it took to conquer the intricacies of the tabla and become an accomplished drummer was required to conquer the intricacies of the personality and become a Soul-guided human being.

Peter was given compositions during his lessons, but he had to coach himself to adjust during his practice, to correct mistakes, and to fine-tune his body and mind.

I saw myself in Peter's dedication to his music and realized how we must coach ourselves on the field of life like master musicians in training. We must dedicate ourselves to the sacred task of transforming our personality and our life, so that the enlightened aspects of our Soul shines through us into the world.

Peter eventually left Petaluma and went back to live in Marin, but he visited us frequently throughout his teenage years. Peter and I continued to build a friendship, staying awake until the wee hours of the morning, listening to music and laughing and joking.

Many evenings when everyone else fell asleep, Peter would practice compositions over and over, and like a human metronome, I would keep the cycle of 16 beats for him on my hand by using my thumb to count four beats on each finger.

This was not easy, because the rhythm patterns he played were syncopated and extremely complicated. During these sessions, it became apparent that, by tuning into that certain centered place within my being that I had found during prayer and my meditation sessions, I was able to keep the beat for extended periods of time without getting thrown off. As a result, Peter always liked it when I kept "tal" for him.

Studying Western music at the time, my only exposure to teaching had been through written music. So, this method of teaching by recitation was intriguing.

I made every effort to convince my parents to let me move from Sonoma State and spend my college fund at the Ali Akbar College. After several discussions, even soliciting the help of a psychologist, my parents finally agreed. However, I was to pay for my first semester on my own.

I spent the summer living with the Huichol Indians, learning new embroidery skills from the women and the art of yarn painting from a Huichol medicine man, Raymundo. He taught me all that was needed to create and sell a yarn painting collection of my own, providing me with the money to study tabla at the Ali Akbar College.

While looking for a place to rent with several other musicians from the college, fate stepped in and I found a house right down the street from where Zakir and Pete lived in San Geronimo— another sign from the universe that I was on the right track.

It was during this time, in 1976, that Zakir and Micky Hart founded the Diga Rhythm Band. Two of my roommates and close friends were in the band, Tor Dietrichson on tabla and Ray Spiegel on vibes. A pay phone was installed in our living room to communicate rehearsal schedules with "the boys." My job was to drive everyone to Mickey Hart's studio, the Barn, in Novato, California, to rehearse and record the album. There were six tabla players in the band, and I watched, mesmerized, as Zakir beautifully orchestrated the tabla ensemble and created spellbinding rhythms with Mickey and the band.

During my classes at the college, I was grateful to sit with Zakir for both private and group lessons. One-on-one, he taught me with unending patience as I learned the rhythm cycles of 7 beats (Rupak), 10 beats (Jhap tal), as well as the traditional 16 beats (Tin tal). In group lessons, Zakir always called on me and encouraged me to join in as I learned the tabla compositions and became more fluent at playing them on my drums.

Peter was an advanced student, so we never crossed paths in class. However, social events were a different story.

Peter Peringer was a one-man show, and wherever he went he made people laugh. We often gathered together with groups of our AACM friends, and Pete's comedic gifts were the highlight of every party. When Peter was in a crowd, it was as if he was on stage. He would take situations from daily life and improvise parodies in Jhap tal. He'd make up two or three verses on the spot, fit them perfectly into the rhythm cycle, and have everyone doubled over with laughter in a matter of minutes. He'd even use the top of people's heads as drums, and they loved it!

Peter's passion for Indian music was unquenchable, and wherever he went, he inspired people with his insatiable will to practice his art. When he wasn't practicing, he was in the hallways at the college or on the streets in town reciting intricate compositions in the syncopated rhythm cycles that flowed from him in a way that was unfathomable to others.

One night, Pete and I drove into town to the house of another friend, Michael Luchessa, who also went to the Ali Akbar College of Music. He lived in a white two-story house on an acre of property in Fairfax. Michael was from a true Italian family, and this house was his grandparents' summer home. Michael's dad had actually lived there in the summers while dating Michael's mom.

The house was built in the 1930s and had ornate molding around the ceilings and doors. In the center was a large living room with beautiful hardwood floors and a tall, molded ceiling. There was a painted brick fireplace against one wall, and antique furniture that had been passed down for generations.

Several students from the college rented the three bedrooms that surrounded the living room. One night, we were all listening to music when everyone went to sleep except Peter and me. We sat in two large deep brown velvet antique chairs, with the only source of light coming from the fireplace. A warm glow filled the room when another extraordinary event struck again.

Closing our eyes, we savored with intense concentration the musical genius of Carlos Santana's *Caravanserai*.

Somehow, this spontaneous meditation facilitated an alignment with an exquisite energy—it washed through us in waves, sweeping us along on currents of feeling, carrying us to that place of power within where we merged with an energy transcending the physical body and world. Then we were lifted up in our Soul bodies. I felt the angelic energy I had experienced in Honey and Janet's presence—the energy of our Souls.

We looked down, amazed, on the beautiful shells of living flesh that we had temporarily vacated. From this vantage point, it seemed that anything was possible.

This happened in a flash, but the entire episode seemed eternal. Then, as soon as the music ended, without warning we were jolted back into our physical bodies.

We just sat there, speechless. It took a while to even be able to move our hands. Finally, I gasped, "Did you feel that?"

"Did you see what I saw?" Peter cried out, almost in shock. "Oh my God, what was that? I was looking down at my body from up above it!"

I exclaimed, "So was I," not fully understanding what had actually happened.

Pete and I began laughing, first out of amazement and then half-hysterically, because it was so unexpected. Both of our bodies felt like lead weights, and it took us a while before we were able to walk to the door and drive home.

A seed had been planted, for Pete was now 19 years old and this was just the first of many extraordinary experiences that Peter and I were to have together.

But why and how had this happened?

Somehow, we had aligned with the currents of energy that surround the earth and every living thing and had touched the source of unlimited possibilities. It wasn't a physical place we had gone to, but a state of consciousness, of oneness with the Soul!

This event left me wanting to know more. When we ask, we had better be ready to receive! So, I asked the universe again, "Show me more about how these powers and newfound insights can be applied in common, everyday interactions with others, in the here and now!"

The very next day I contacted my close friend, Elaine, to see if there was any way she could give me a ride to the airport. It was too expensive to leave my car there. I was hoping she would do me this favor since I had given her numerous rides over the last few years.

When I walked into her house, she was busy taking care of chores as she had always done, her long brown hair disheveled. To my surprise, Elaine squinted her dark piercing eyes and curtly replied, "No, I really can't today, I have to do laundry."

I left feeling a great deal of anger and resentment at what I thought was Elaine's selfishness. Then I recalled how, just the night before, I had been lifted out of my body in an angelic form, looked down at myself from above, and felt the universal energy that was the essence of my Soul. Here I was now, grinding my teeth, angry at another Soul who was trapped in her personality.

"Okay, Cindy," I coached myself, "there must be a way to view this situation in a different light. I don't have to identify with my lower personality that is creating these emotions and be trapped in its drama. I can tune in to something deeper and wiser. I can shift to my Soul's viewpoint and observe this moment objectively, from a more enlightened perspective."

I took a few moments, closed my eyes, and followed my own advice. As I tuned in and let go, I felt a sense of release. I was able to see more clearly the absurdity of the situation with Elaine. I became a calm observer of the situation, rather than an agitated participant. As my attachment to being right dissolved, a vision presented itself of who I wanted to be in the situation. It was vastly different than who I had been up until a few moments ago. Was this my higher purpose? It seemed so.

The first thought that raced into my mind, since I had been raised Episcopalian, was an adaptation of what Jesus said on the Cross: "Forgive her, for she knows not what she does."

That was it! In her own mind she was justified, and nothing could change that, no matter how unjust it felt to me. That was the reality of her world, which I was not to judge.

As I moved from the emotion of anger to a more enlightened feeling of calm, from holding on to letting go, I was freed. I had just exercised the power of my own Soul in every-day life to choose the world I would live in.

In that moment, newfound insights solidified. It is our job to choose our thoughts and perspectives, for they form our experience of reality. The difference between Heaven and Hell was simply a difference between two vantage points—that of our limited personality, and that of our eternal Soul.

Enlightenment, it seemed, could be attained through daily practice during personal challenges—by a simple shift in consciousness, from identification with the voice of our limited human personality, to identification with the voice of our eternal Soul.

This was our higher purpose!

With Elaine not willing and me forgiving her, now my only option left was to hitchhike from San Rafael to the San

Francisco Airport, about a 45-minute journey across the Golden Gate Bridge and through the foggy city. It was getting late, and as a young girl traveling alone, this was not an ideal situation. Standing in San Rafael at the entrance to Hwy 101, I fervently called out to the universe, "Please get me to the airport safely!"

Within a matter of minutes, a green Volvo pulled over up ahead—not at all miraculous. However, once I could see in the car, I discovered that the driver of the car was Elaine's own sister, also a friend of mine. Better yet, she happily offered to drive me all the way to the airport. Not a word was mentioned about my frustration with Elaine. I was safe and comfortable. I had transformed my anger and was content in the moment.

A few months after Peter and my extraordinary out-of-body episode, I decided to move into Fairfax and rented a room in Michael's house. Then the miracle happened.

CHAPTER 12

The Hexagonal Ring

Michael and I became great friends, dated for a brief time, and in the summer of 1976, we were married. I was 24 years old, and Michael was 25. The wedding was our version of an American Indian ceremony, held in the side yard of the Fairfax house. It was a spiritual ceremony, complete with a fire in the center of a medicine wheel made from red earth.

My bridesmaids were women of the six directions, who each carried a gift that was placed in the fire as prayers were spoken aloud. My dad walked me around the path of the medicine wheel in his suit and tie, and then gave me away.

My wedding gown was a cotton dress I had purchased in Greece while on my way to Israel. It was decorated with the Sioux Indian Black Elk's vision that I had embroidered while living on the kibbutz. Michael wore a buckskin shirt he had made, with bead work that I had woven onto the sleeves. His thick beard, curly brown hair, and dark Italian skin even made him look the part.

A little over a year later, I gave birth to our daughter, Tamarin Angelique Luchessa.

We were proud parents, and it was amazing to think that her home birth was in the Fairfax house, the very same home, with a fire in the very same fireplace, where Peter and I had shared our out-of-body experience.

When Tamarin was just hours old, Pete put her on his lap and played tabla rhythms to her while he recited compositions into her newborn ear. This was just the beginning of a wonderful bond that grew over the years between Pete and Tamarin.

When Tam was a few months old, we visited with Zakir and his wife Antonia Minnecola (Toni) at their home in San Anselmo. Zakir played tabla for Tamarin while she lay on the carpet in front of his drums. Not yet able to crawl, Tam lifted her head and with blue eyes as big as saucers, absorbed every drum pattern, every rhythm Zakir played deep into her Soul.

Zakir, Toni, and their two kids, Anisa and Isabella, became great friends of ours over the years. Toni is a leading exponent of Kathak, the classical dance style of North India. She is the disciple of the late, legendary Sitara Devi, who is considered the greatest female Kathak dancer of our time.

Often, I would play tabla for the Kathak classes taught by Chitresh Das at AACM. Toni studied with Chitresh for many years at the beginning of her Kathak career and watching her train with the other dancers truly inspired me.

So, I decided to switch from studying Tabla to Kathak, eventually becoming a Kathak dancer in the Chitresh Das Dance Company. It was an exciting time, as we often performed at the Herbst Theatre in San Francisco and other local venues. Michael eventually started a business as a carpenter and left the AACM. While deep into motherhood, I held odd jobs and still managed to practice and perform Kathak.

After four years, however, my marriage to Michael dissolved and I moved to Los Angeles for the summer to be closer to my family.

Eventually, I moved back to Marin, and Michael and I were able to establish a good co-parenting relationship with Tamarin. I rented a house in San Anselmo with friends and fellow Kathak dancers. Peter and I remained close during this time, and he eventually moved into our rental with two of his friends.

Our relationship grew even stronger over time, and our deep friendship gradually took a turn toward love. Soon, our evening talks became romantic talks and the energy between us ignited quickly. Everyone realized we were more than just friends—this was a fun time in both of our lives.

Peter, now 24 years old, stood 5'10" with a thick, powerful build and a hefty hug. His sculptured features were more manly, and his curly brown hair was now short, yet thick and full—still reminding me of Michelangelo's David.

Tamarin had just turned 5 years old, and it was time that I move out and buy a place of my own. I purchased a condominium nearby, and Peter eventually moved in with us. We had been living together there for four years when the next extraordinary event occurred.

One morning, we woke up next to one another, holding hands. We looked over, smiled at each other, and then closed our eyes as if to go back to sleep. Within a few minutes, we were both holding hands, but this time we were floating above our bodies, looking down on ourselves again!

This experience also felt like an eternity but lasted for only a few minutes.

Astonished, we looked at each other as Peter said, "Did you feel what I felt?"

I told him what I had seen, and he said, "Oh my God, me too!"

We reflected on the experience we had years earlier while listening to Santana and marveled at the coincidence that this had just happened to us a second time. We felt grateful that our energies were in tune with one another, and we were able to share this experience.

We now had many traditions together, and French toast on Sunday morning was a special one.

Peter woke up especially early one Sunday morning and made his famous French toast. We were having a fun time laughing and eating breakfast together when he looked over at me with a rare serious look on his face.

With a loving tone in his voice, Pete grabbed my hand and asked, "Will you marry me?"

I was surprised by his sudden request, and immediately said, "Yes."

As our marriage plans unfolded, Peter took me shopping for a ring. It was important to him that we picked out the ring together. We found a beautiful ring right away, but we both felt it was not the ring. So, we decided to take it slow until we found one that we both really loved.

Three days later, I came home from work and Peter said he had something to show me. "Had Pete gone shopping and found a ring he really liked?" I silently wondered.

Peter disappeared into the other room, and I felt sure that whatever ring he had picked out would be fine with me. He returned with a big smile on his face.

I was delighted to see Pete pull a blue velvet ring box out of a mailer, but it was puzzling as to why it had been sent in the mail. Those questions disappeared instantly, as Peter's infectious enthusiasm enveloped me. Before he would let me see the ring, Pete explained the circumstances leading up to this moment with an energy that was thoroughly captivating.

It turned out that Pete's mom had sent him her engagement ring from his dad.

Pete was so excited at the idea of me having his mom's ring that he couldn't restrain himself. At the same time, he insisted on saying, "Lu, you do not have to keep this ring. If you don't like it, we will find another one."

Well, there was no question. I thought it was incredibly special as well, particularly because Pete's dad had died of a brain tumor and was no longer with us. In pure Peter-fashion, he still wouldn't show the ring to me until he had told me not only the entire build up, but also every conceivable way out if I didn't like it.

By now the anticipation was unbearable, and I begged Peter, "I love the idea, I really love the idea. Please open the box."

Pete obliged, but the box seemed to open in slow motion. Peering through his fingers, I struggled to get any glimpse at all of what was inside.

As Peter turned the box in my direction to finally show me the ring, I shrieked!

The ring Peter's mom had sent us was a silver baguette diamond, cut into a hexagonal shape—exactly like the ring Janet had shown me.

It was also the very same ring I had sketched in my journal 12 years earlier.

I was stunned.

Peter kept saying, "What, Lu, what?"

He knew the story of Janet telling me to leave Israel, so once I regained my composure, I told him how she had also shown me a hexagonal-shaped ring that was to bring new understandings. I told Peter that I loved the ring, and then ran over to the closet and retrieved my journal, where the ring had been prominently sketched.

Now it was Peter who was stunned.

We hugged for what seemed like an eternity, and words were no longer necessary.

Pete was so glad that the ring was a keeper. I wanted some gold in my wedding band, so we decided to design gold around the diamonds in the engagement ring. As it turned out, Peter's ring was designed to match mine, and we both ended up wearing hexagonal-shaped wedding rings.

An even bigger picture had now presented itself, and Janet's messages made even more sense. It was all a miracle.

Not only was I to go back home and be spared the rigors of an imminent war, but I was also to move to Northern California, study Indian music, give birth to Tamarin, and, lastly, meet and fall in love with Peter.

How could this all be planned 12 years before it happened? It was becoming more and more evident that there was a plan for my life, and my grandmother had access to what my future held. But if there was a plan, how could I become aware of it—or was I already?

Only one mystery remained from Janet's three messages. The hexagonal ring represented our union, but how was that equated with new understandings?

I asked Peter what he thought, and he replied, "Maybe new understandings about love?" Yes, that was a clever way to look at it, but in reality, I still did not know the true meaning of Janet's statement, "From this ring will come new understandings."

Pete and I were married in an intimate ceremony at my mom's house in Westwood, CA. Dad and Jeanne came over from their house nearby in Brentwood, and Tamarin, now 7 years old, was our ring bearer. Debby was living in New York, and she and her wife, Carol, flew out to be there. Peter's mom, sister, and brother-in-law also travelled to be there with us.

The ceremony was short and lovely. It was conducted by the same preacher who had baptized me, Debby, and Tamarin. This made the day even more special.

Once back in Northern California, we hosted a wonderful reception with 60 of our friends and music family. Peter played timbales while our friend Ray played vibes and Tor played congas as we all danced together and had a wonderful time.

The friendships we had from the Ali Akbar College were so special to us, and it was amazing to continually witness the love we all had for one another; especially the love everyone had for Pete. It is hard to describe the rare power that he had, the instant connection Pete made with people, his warmth, gentleness, intelligence, sense of humor, and his rare capacity to give and receive love.

Peter's life was exceptional and graced, yet it was not without its trials and tribulations.

Yes, Pete had an uncanny gift for entertaining, but on the other side of the coin, this gift was also his challenge. He could be the life of the party one minute, but if someone said or did something that bothered him, he didn't know how to tell them. And he couldn't let it go. It would build up in his mind for days, causing him and those around him a great deal of anxiety and despair.

These mood swings that plagued him were known mostly to those closest to him, and they were often stressful to manage. I would do my best to paint a positive perspective, but not always successfully.

Like the flip of a switch, Pete could be angry and upset at home, and then we'd meet up with friends, and within minutes, he'd make an entire group of people dissolve into hysterical fits of laughter. As a result, Pete was everyone's best friend.

While Peter's gift was his music, another challenge he faced was wanting desperately to be a businessman like his father, who inherited a family wheat farm and transformed it into a multi-property wheat and grass seed business. Pete's music hadn't satisfied this entrepreneurial urge.

Zakir frequently encouraged Peter to tour, but Pete didn't want a touring lifestyle. He loved his home, family, and hanging out with his friends. Peter had musician friends who also maintained business careers. From talking with them, he realized the disconcerting factor that prevented him from achieving business success: his lack of education.

Peter had been one of those gifted children who had difficulty with conventional classroom environments. Inspired to help Pete, his parents had started a free school in Spokane, Washington. During the early seventies it provided a perfect open environment for learning.

Then, Pete left his home at 13 years old to study drumming in the Bay Area. Peter's formal, structured education only went through the sixth grade. As a result, he was insecure about his ability to read.

My efforts to encourage Pete to develop his reading skills were unsuccessful. He could only focus for a brief time until frustration stopped him short. To become a traditional businessman meant he would have to go back to school. That was not an option for Pete.

Peter had received a trust fund after his father's death, so money wasn't an issue. Yet this inheritance became both a blessing and a curse. The blessing was obvious. The curse was Peter's habit of lending money to friends and acquaintances who often didn't pay it back. The resulting sense of betrayal exacerbated the mood swings that afflicted Peter's life. Over time his self-destructive generosity destroyed his sense of well-being.

Then came "D-Day," as I called it because the bombs began to drop all around Peter.

He was struggling after yet another friend he had lent money to disappeared. Pete managed to cope through the weekend, but by Monday the betrayal had eaten away his peace and left him in a state of obsession. That morning I was more forceful than usual in trying to get Peter to focus on positive solutions. I urged him to reconsider building a career with his music, reminding him of Zakir's invitations to go on tour and of other musicians who wanted him to perform with them. His extraordinary gift was the envy of many successful drummers. Yet touring and working night clubs was not what Peter wanted.

Deep down, he feared failing and was frustrated with the basic level of security his trust fund provided.

That morning, I felt Pete's Soul slipping into the familiar darkness of this problem. He didn't want me telling him what to do, and I was pushing too hard. An argument ensued, and we both knew it was time to take a break.

Peter left the house to stay with his sister, Pam, and we didn't see each other for five days. It was the longest we'd been away from each other in years.

We spoke on the phone once. In that conversation, Peter told me he had fainted in the bathroom. This incident frightened both of us and initiated his sudden return home.

The evening of his return, we talked for hours and came to an understanding.

During dinner, Peter asked me to give him six months to figure out his life direction. He admitted that he was self-destructing and needed to get help to deal with the ups and downs in his life. The evening felt like a significant turning point for both of us.

At one point, after many hours of lengthy discussions, Peter came up behind me, kissed my cheek, and rubbed my hand. "I love you, Lu," he whispered as our bodies melted together.

The next morning something very odd happened. Peter seemed unusually pale. At one point we embraced and gazed sweetly into each other's eyes as Peter gently held my face in his hands.

"Do you know why I left the house?" he suddenly asked. "Maybe in some way I'm preparing you for when I die young. It won't be so hard on you once it happens."

Stunned, I backed away. For a moment I was speechless. We'd only been married for seven months. Peter had said several times over the years that he had a weird feeling he wasn't supposed going to be alive long. He had disturbing dreams of dying young, leaving his family and friends grieving.

I didn't believe it would happen because Peter was such a good person. Now, for the first time, I felt the fear that his premonitions might be true, but I quickly brushed it away.

"Pete," I said with sweet assurance, "You're such a great guy, you'll probably outlive me."

That weekend, Tamarin and I had planned to visit with Mom and Debby in L.A.

The morning we left, Peter called out to me from the shower, "Will you get some clothes out for me?"

He loved having me pick out his clothes, and I loved doing it. I laid out his grey corduroy pants and white "Jazzercise" t-shirt. Yet all that morning I was filled with apprehension. Peter sensed it too. Our good-bye hug was unusual; like a hug you would give to someone who was going off to war or going on a dangerous mission. It was a hug that said, "I don't want you to go, but I know you have to. I'm afraid I may never see you again."

Here we were, standing at the front door on our way to L.A. for the weekend, and we couldn't stop hugging. 8-year-old Tamarin was clasping our legs, her long blonde hair almost touching her knees as she tilted her head back to look up at us, to say goodbye to her Papa Pete.

The look in Peter's beautiful amber eyes that morning was unforgettable. They peered deep into my Soul with that radiant, loving gleam that had crowned my heart for many years. Cupping my face in his hands once again, Peter smiled and said curiously, "Look at us, we can't stop hugging and you're only going away for the weekend!"

So much love was exchanged on that doorstep. We bathed in a sense of eternity, and it felt as if lifetimes had led up to this moment. We finally released each other, yet we kept our eyes fixed on one another all the way down the stairs to the car.

As Tamarin and I drove away, a gut-wrenching fear ripped through me like a streaking bullet. "What was that?" I wondered.

My concerns were alleviated by Tamarin's exuberant little face smiling with delight. She had felt the love in that parting moment. As I once again focused on the warm feelings of our embrace, a sense of peace returned.

CHAPTER 13

Divine Design

Iwas excited to see Debby in L.A. After leaving Sonoma State she got her MFA degree at UCLA, and while visiting Santa Barbara she had met Carol. They moved to New York, and Debby was now building a career selling commercial airtime in Manhattan.

Although she will always live with the knowledge that at any time complications from Lupus could flare up, Debby moved forward with strength and conviction. She settled into her life in Brooklyn, found a new doctor in Manhattan, and adapted a regimen of Chinese herbs along with her medications.

Upon our arrival in L.A., Mom greeted Tam and I at the door. The smell of her famous chili simmering on the stove wafted through the air. Debby had arrived earlier that day, so we made drinks, and all went and sat down together in the living room.

Mom, or Grammy as Tam called her, had given Tamarin a new *My Little Pony* set, so Tam went into the den to play with it. During the drive to L.A., I had reflected on the fact that I hadn't yet talked to my family about my deep-seated feeling of abandonment while they were caring for Debby during her illness. It seemed that the time to do so had arrived.

The now familiar voice of my Soul communicated to me, "Part of embracing your difficult, deep-rooted thoughts and emotions is sharing them with others. Then you can release them and make room for higher wisdom."

Despite the familiar fears, I knew it was time. "Oh, brother," I thought. "Here we go again, another scary conversation."

As Mom and Debby conversed back and forth, I was still feeling reluctant to share my feelings. My fears were telling me not to risk ruining the nice evening we had planned. On the other hand, my intuition, the voice of my Soul, was telling me that it was the right thing to do.

With the gourmet smells of mom's chili filling the room, I took a breath and blurted out, "You guys, I have to talk to you about something!"

Mom quickly lit a Sherman cigarette, sensing that something was up. Debby crossed her long, thin legs against the couch and her dark serious eyes told me I had her complete attention.

Before I could say another word, I burst out crying. I started talking through my tears, unable to contain myself as I shared with my mom and sister my feelings of abandonment, held inside for so many years.

Mom and Debby sat silent, staring at me open-mouthed, their eyes full of surprise and sympathy.

"Oh, Cindy!" Mom said, deeply moved. "I always wondered how that all affected you. I felt so badly, but I didn't know if I should bring it up. I didn't want to raise an issue if there wasn't one, so I was reluctant to ask."

That moment was extremely healing. Mom had truly heard me.

She had always been so understanding and supportive with the big issues in life. Why was I afraid it would be different now? I could see that she, like me, had her own fears and doubts that had held her back. No doubt Dad had, as well.

We had all suffered. No one was at fault. Their youngest daughter had been diagnosed with a terminal illness. Mom and Dad had managed the best they could at the time.

I felt a willingness, a need, to forgive and let it all go. I was not responsible for what happened to me in my childhood. I was accountable, however, for my present choice to either hold onto or release my emotions once they entered the realm of my experience.

I went over and hugged Mom with all my might. My feelings of abandonment suddenly transformed into a sense of overwhelming contentment.

Debby watched me, her face beaming with sudden insight. "Cindy," she said, "I always hated the attention I got and felt bad for you. Maybe this is why you were rebellious as a kid. You were left alone, and you were trying to get the attention you desperately needed."

Yes, that made so much sense. At that moment I knew my troubled teenage years were really a desperate search for attention.

We all stood up for a group hug and gratitude filled the air between us.

Years of baggage seemed lifted from me. Less burdened by my past, I felt free to move on. What a marvelous conversation it had been. Having shared my deepest feelings, secrets, and fears with my family, I had begun to heal old childhood wounds and bridge family gaps.

We had bonded at a deeper level than ever before.

Our dinner was fabulous. Mom being a gourmet cook, had even made Debby a vegetarian version of her chili dish. The conversations while we ate were filled with fun stories and lots of laughter.

However, by the end of our meal I began to feel a penetrating pain in my ear that worsened throughout the night.

The next morning, I awoke early to drive Mom to work. After my parents' divorce, Mom built a career at Neiman-Marcus in couture. She really knew her stuff, and having grown up in L.A., her list of regular clients soon bordered on spectacular. She'd even been written up in an L.A. Times article entitled "The Dressing Room Diva."

By the time I dropped mom off, the pain in my ear had become unbearable. So, I raced to the nearest pay phone, called Bettye for the name of an ear, nose, and throat specialist, scheduled an emergency appointment, and I drove directly to the doctor's office.

The doctor diagnosed an acute ear infection and prescribed antibiotics and codeine. The pain was getting worse by the minute.

While waiting for my prescription to be filled, I went to the magazine and paperback section of the pharmacy and scanned the available books. I came across *Wired: The Short Life and Fast Times of John Belushi* by Bob Woodward.

Over the next two days, Wired was a diversion from my pain. I read the book voraciously, but soon realized that this portrait focused heavily on the destructive qualities of John Belushi rather than also elaborating on his extraordinary gifts. So, while reading each story, I personally reflected on the wonderful heart and soul of John Belushi, who I didn't know, but greatly admired.

Reading Wired made Peter seem a little closer. The more I read, the more the similarities and ironic parallels between these two intense and gifted personalities became apparent. Peter loved John Belushi, looked like John Belushi, lived with the same driven, free-spirit intensity, and had similar comedic gifts. Both were dedicated to their craft, maintained epic friendships, and were loved my many.

John Belushi's story caught me up in an involuntary flow of flashbacks, with a corresponding sense of Pete's own unique personal legacy. One act from Peter's repertoire was "The Motorcycle." Placing his lips to his palm, Pete would make a flap-like sound that he perfected to such a degree that really did sound exactly like a motorcycle, starting, revving up, and roaring off into the distance.

He had a rare ability to turn any situation into a comedy act. He always knew how to play to his audience; how, through a joke or a play on words, to touch the core of a person's Soul, make them feel happy, appreciated, and cared for. Peter's humor came from the same vein as John Belushi, whom he loved to watch on *Saturday Night Live.*

Having met Peter when he was so young, it was amazing to reflect on how we had known each other as good friends, spiritual buddies, lovers, husband and wife, and teachers to one another. Peter often showered me with love. It didn't matter where we were when the feeling took him. In a market, in the car, in a group of people, Peter didn't hesitate to lean over and earnestly kiss me on the lips. When these moments spontaneously occurred, I basked in their glow.

Drunk with memories, I reflected on the power of his complex and remarkable spirit and personality. I felt my love for him and my gratitude for our love, which spanned the gamut of the relationship spectrum, high and low.

Yet part of me wondered why these overpowering reflections were suddenly welling up in me. So, even as my heart and Soul simply flowed with them, I also felt a bit uneasy.

It was now mid-morning, and in the midst of this journey down memory lane, the phone rang. I was surprised and happy to hear the voice of Peter's sister, Pam. I was also concerned as to why she might be calling.

Pam told me that she was worried about Peter. She had called the condo that day, but Peter hadn't answered, and she was scared. I had talked to him the night before, and he sounded in good spirits. I told her there was probably nothing to worry about, that I was confident everything was fine, and I'd be home soon.

However, the severity of my ear infection worsened. When it came time to leave, my doctor warned me not to get on a plane. Tamarin had to fly home alone to Michael's house so she could return to school. Debby flew back to New York.

Then an allergic reaction to codeine in the middle of the night caused me to become violently ill. The next day, the doctor examined me and found so much infection that an immediate in-house operation was required. After the operation, I returned to Mom's house with Vicodin instead of codeine, and with oil that had to be heated and placed in my ears four times a day.

Reading *Wired* was the only high point of the day, as the images of John's loving nature and larger-than-life persona continued to remind me of Peter.

Then I reached the place where, on March 5, 1982, John Belushi died at the Chateau Marmont Hotel on Sunset Boulevard in L.A. The tragedy of this brilliant life and unnecessary death struck me with overwhelming force. Upon reading those passages, I broke down and sobbed, gripped by a dark premonition that my life as I knew it would never be the same.

I remembered the ominous feelings, that internal sonar that had come to me in the past, warning me of terrible events to come. Then I remembered my last conversation with Pam, and panic set in.

I immediately called home, but Peter wasn't there. Next, I called one of Pete's close friends. Toning down the panic in my voice, I asked if he'd seen Pete. It turned out that Peter had spent the night there, and besides worrying about me getting better, Pete was doing good.

So, I hung up the phone somewhat at ease, but my internal sonar was sounding off louder than ever. The date was March 2, 1985. The time was approximately 3:00 in the afternoon.

With Mom working and having to care for me at night, it was time to give her a break. I made arrangements for Dad to come pick me up so I could stay with him and Jeanne for a while.

Jeanne was not just a stepmother to me. Having lived with her off and on during my teens while my parents cared for Debby, she was more of a mother figure. I felt incredibly grateful to be able to stay with Dad and Jeanne at their home.

Now alone in their kitchen, all the fear and pain of the last few days, and the terror of my premonitions, hit me with sudden force. I simply broke down and cried standing there, alone in the kitchen. "What's going to happen next?" I wailed, leaning weakly against the counter. "Is someone that I love going to die?"

Dad came in and held me as we talked for a while. I told him what was going on within me, about the impact reading about John Belushi's life and death, and my fears of impending tragedy.

In my father's arms and comforting presence, a sense of calm returned.

That night, I sat in the living room with Dad and Jeanne watching *Murder, She Wrote*. At the peak of the suspense, just as Angela Lansbury was about to solve the murder in the bathroom, our telephone rang.

No one wanted to answer it. The phone kept ringing and ringing. We all expected that whoever it was would hang up and call again later. But the ringing didn't stop.

"Maybe it's Mom," I said.

Jumping up, I ran to answer it. The phone was down the hall in the master bedroom. I turned the corner into the darkness. With the lights off, my eyes had not yet adjusted. I was also disoriented from my medication, and it was hard to see even a foot in front of me.

All this time the phone was still ringing on the small antique table by the side of my parents' bed. Fumbling in the dark while looking for a phone that kept ringing, I felt as if I was wandering through some sort of illogical time warp.

Finally, I found the receiver and picked it up.

"Hello," I said cautiously while taking a seat at the edge of the antique four-poster bed.

"Hello, Cindy, this is Michael," the voice on the other end of the line said pointedly.

Tamarin's dad was the last person I expected to hear from.

"Michael, what's wrong? Is Tamarin all right?"

Michael paused, took a deep breath, and said, painfully, "Cindy, there's been a problem with Pete."

"What?" my body instantly froze. "What happened?"

"I don't know," Michael said. "There's a policeman here who wants to talk to you."

Before I could prepare myself, a strange monotone voice came on the line.

"Mrs. Peringer?" it said, matter-of-factly.

"Yes."

"Are you the wife of Peter Peringer?"

"Yes, where is he? What's wrong?" I was in a total panic.

"He's dead."

I went numb. "What...where?" I stammered.

"At the Clarion Hotel, Ma'am," the flat voice said.

"The Clarion Hotel? How?" I asked now in shock.

"We do not know that at this time."

I could no longer speak. Now, for the first time, there was a note of compassion in the voice.

"Are you all right, Ma'am?"

"Well...no!" I blurted.

"Are you alone?"

"No, my parents are here." I answered.

"Can I speak with them?"

At that, I literally threw down the phone and ran toward the light coming from the living room, yelling in an animal-like primal wail, "Dad!!!!"

I saw looks of horror on Dad and Jeanne's faces as I reached out to them screaming, "Peter's dead, Peter's dead!!!"

Collapsing into Jeanne's arms, I begged Dad to go to the phone. Somehow, I ended up curled in her arms like a fetus, sobbing uncontrollably, my whole body aching in the grip of an appalling horror.

I cried out, "What is happening?" It felt like I was struggling to wake from a nightmare.

I tried to think rationally for a moment. "What should I do?" I wondered.

The immediate priority, I realized, was to call Peter's family and to let my mom know. Luckily, my parents were all still friends, so Mom was out the door to Dad and Jeanne's the moment I told her.

I struggled to pull myself together. I had to find out what had happened and decide what to do next. We all spent the rest of the evening trying to get information, talking to the coroner's office, and dealing with the shock of Peter's death as best we could.

That night, as my strength wavered with the unfolding details of this tragedy, my family supported and protected me with their love. Luckily, Tamarin was asleep at her dad's and was sheltered from this tragic event until I could get home to tell her the news—her Papa was no longer with us.

The first information the coroner's office relayed to us was that Peter had died while getting ready to take a shower at the hotel. The maid had walked into his room the next morning and found him lying on the bathroom floor with the shower running.

In one way this was eerie since a few weeks earlier Peter had feared fainting in the bathroom. In another way, it was oddly comforting. Peter loved taking showers and called them his meditation. The last thing he did before we left for L.A. was, take a shower.

Next, the coroner told us that Peter had checked into the Clarion Hotel on March 3, 1985, at 6:30 p.m., only a day after Pam's concerned phone call, and only hours after I had broken down reading about John Belushi's death at the Chateau

Marmont Hotel and made my frantic call home to find Peter.

The synchronicities of these events instilled a sense of destiny within me, but I was overcome by grief and filled with guilt. "Could I have prevented this tragedy if my ear infection had not kept me bedridden," I wondered. "Or, better yet, if I had not even traveled to L.A.?"

In those hours after learning of Peter's death, I struggled with the way it had all come about. Bottom line is, we will never know why Pete was at a hotel, or what the set of circumstances of that early evening were.

More importantly, I did begin to realize one thing. Premonitory experiences and practical events beyond anyone's control had allowed Peter's passing to unfold exactly as planned—by divine design.

An odd sense of appreciation, even gratitude, rose in me. I began to feel that there was nothing random in his death or the circumstances surrounding it. My Soul told me it had been fated, as Peter himself had said more than once. Even the fact that I had been at home with my family who could care for me in the aftermath of this tragedy seemed serendipitous.

Amongst my shock and grief resided a sense that Pete's death, and the experiences leading up to it, had unfolded perfectly according to a higher plan. At that moment all of the inexplicable events of my life seemed verify one simple truth—we live not by chance, but by divine design.

It was now past midnight and we had done all we could do, said all we could say, and cried all we could cry for one evening. Mom went home, and the time had come for me to try and get some sleep.

Exhausted and apprehensive, I went alone into the guest room and shut the sliding door behind me.

PART 4
MESSAGES FROM THE AFTERLIFE

CHAPTER 14

The New Understandings

I lay in the dark with the music of Santana softly reverberating through the room, afraid to close my eyes for fear of envisioning the tragedy of Peter's last moments.

In my pain and sorrow, I once again silently cried out for help. I prayed from the depths of my being for Peter's spirit to be surrounded by light and visualized a white light enveloping him. I prayed for him to be taken to the highest place possible and begged the angels in higher realms to come and assist him in his time of crossing over.

Then I prayed for myself—I prayed to be healed of my own shock and despair.

Yes, I had found that prayer and meditation gave me strength and peace in the face of the tragedies that had engulfed my life. Yet, this time, I was in more pain and grief than I had ever imagined possible. I felt as if I, too, was dying, so I urgently cried out for help from a depth in myself that I had never known.

Then, something extraordinary occurred.

Within moments, a whirling ball of light encircled the room. An electrical current pulsed throughout my body, accompanied by a loud buzzing in my ears.

The sensations merged and formed a low vibrating pitch at the base of my spine. Then it began to ascend, moving up the musical scale as it rose through my body, whirling faster and faster, sounding higher and higher around and through my pelvis, my stomach, my heart, my throat, and my forehead. When it reached the top of my head, the tone had become a high-pitched Tibetan bell-like whine.

The vibrational intensity increased to what felt like the speed of light. Involuntarily drawn into the magnetic vibrations, I was transported in a subtler and finer body, my Soul body, through a void into the serene vastness of the universe.

At first, I saw millions of small balls of light everywhere, like golden stars and tiny planets, emerging from the pitch blackness.

Then suddenly, a Romanesque temple appeared, with long white stairs and tall marble pillars. Peter was standing on the stairs!

As we started up the steps together, we were instantly transported into a large hall.

There, spiritual beings sat around a long mahogany-like table, intensely bright, with distinctly human forms. Looking like wise sages with golden auras and white robes, they communicated with us telepathically.

Lovingly they said: "Where we are now, this is home. The earth plane is your training ground, your temporary school of life. No matter how hard your lessons or how difficult life becomes, you have chosen to go there to learn from your experiences."

"Together with us you choose your family, your time and place of birth, and the specific situations that will challenge you and give your Soul the best opportunity to evolve."

"In one mortal lifetime, you will attempt to master at the most two or three challenging emotions. Observe yourself in daily life. Get to know who you are. And in the face of difficulties, choose who you want to be."

"Take time each day to go within, charge your system, and cultivate the power of Soul consciousness."

Next, we were taken to another section of the temple where a large screen connected to a massive, sophisticated machine was lowered in front of me.

A view of earth was projected onto the screen, as clear and vivid as if I were looking out at it from a spaceship. The machine attached to the screen directed energy towards earth to uplift its vibratory energy field. I was shown scenes from my life, as if it were a movie, depicting the adversities I'd face and how to manage them.

I was then given more messages: "You are to be a connector between the seen and unseen—between the physical body and the eternal Soul. And through the written word, you will provide the steps necessary to master the higher purpose of life on earth."

Next, we were transported onto a beach. Peter was beside me wearing his blue corduroy pants and the white Puerto Rican-style shirt he liked to wear while playing Timbales. We walked along the ocean holding hands, existing together in a non-physical reality.

Then Peter spoke to me, very directly, lovingly, and reassuringly.

"I am happy," he said. "I am with Cupid, and I am surrounded with a lot of love."

When we looked in each other's eyes, time and space disappeared. The feeling of peace and unconditional love we shared in this higher reality was overwhelming.

Then a building appeared. Peter led me inside again, not through a door. We were simply transported inside. I saw the same spiritual beings as were in the temple. Pete walked towards them and said to me, "I have to go now."

Then he disappeared.

I looked around and saw a sophisticated piece of equipment much like our computer systems, with a printer attached. Our friend Geoffrey was at the console.

"Geoffrey, Geoffrey, quick!" I shouted. "Contact Peter! Contact the spirit world on the computer!"

Geoffrey immediately began typing on the keyboard, and messages came from the printer that said, "I am happy now, I am with Cupid, and I am surrounded by a lot of love. Your prayers have moved me on. I will always love you. Give my love to everyone."

As Peter's farewell resonated throughout my being, the buzzing vibrations once again began to envelop me. Soon, however, their intensity decreased, lowering in pitch until they were no longer audible.

Then I found myself back in my physical body in the darkened room, paralyzed by the tingling energetic sensations that engulfed me. Overwhelming emotions rose from the depths within me, as feelings of awe mingled with my grief over the loss of Pete.

I lay in my bed, marveling at the profundity of the experience. Had our two previous out-of-body experiences prepared us for this? I didn't know for sure, but it felt like they had.

While the experience was fresh in my mind, I wrote down

everything the Beings of Light had said. I had never publicly written anything in my life, but trusted that when the time was right, the way would be shown to me.

I had so many questions. "What does it mean to master my emotions and choose who I want to be?" "How am I supposed to 'charge my system' and 'cultivate the power' of Soul consciousness?"

One thing I did know was that intelligent Beings exist beyond this earth plane.

I had entered a realm of vibrations underlying our visible physical universe and telepathically received messages from Peter and the Beings of Light. I had traveled in my Soul body to dimensions unseen, further confirming that I too am a being of light. I am an eternal Soul, and this essential part of me that survives the death of my physical body is a powerful and intelligent guiding force within me right now.

As I lay there, I reflected how my own trauma and fervent prayers had brought forth the Beings of Light and activated the power of my Soul. The vibrational state of my body went from the low frequencies of trauma and grief to the higher frequencies of Soul consciousness, joy, and indescribable peace and love.

It was the same experience I'd had a few years earlier when a shaman from Brazil had worked my energy field with an instrument much like a piano tuning fork and raised the vibrational level within me.

In much the same way, the Beings of Light, like a tuning fork, had accelerated the energy vibrations within my body, allowing me access to the extraordinary dimension they called home.

My experience left me in a heightened state where I could not sleep. Powerful vibratory sensations still coursed through my body, and a whirling energy sensation was subtly pulsating at the base of my spine. My mind was immersed in new understandings.

I knew from my studies of Laya Yoga that along the spinal cord runs a finer astral cord on which energy centers known as chakras or wheels are threaded. In each center is a latent energy; a potential force that remains inactive until it is awakened and released.

Once released, this energy travels up the astral cord through each of the chakras in ascending pitches, like rising notes on a musical scale, until it reaches the top of and above the head. There in the higher frequencies, intuitive channels are opened up, allowing perceptions beyond the common range of the five senses, beyond space and time.

I couldn't help but wonder how we could benefit from this world of vibrations in a more refined form. How could it be accessed without shock and trauma? I was convinced that there must be a way to harness this energy naturally.

Did I choose this experience of Pete dying as the Beings of Light had said? Was this part of a Soul plan that I created before incarnating?

At one point in this reverie, my mind snapped back to the grim earthly reality of Peter's death and my loss. Darkness engulfed me, and I let myself fall into a well of pain and sorrow that made my body writhe.

Then a stern voice inside me said, "Cindy, pull yourself up, pull yourself out of this."

"How am I supposed to do that?" I wondered silently.

I noticed again the low hum at the base of my spine and focused my attention there. The energy drew me into its vibration.

Soon, my attention moved up my spine to the energy center at my pelvis. There the vibrations rose in pitch and the energy spun faster. My attention rose with the energy and the vibrations to my navel, and on to my heart and my throat. The energy sensations whirled faster and faster, and the pitch rose as if notes on the musical scale were playing C D E F G A B C.

The energy, and my attention, rose into my forehead and up and out the top of my head. I felt a higher force harmonizing the energy of my whole body, gradually transforming my sadness, pain, and anguish into a peaceful calm.

I had spontaneously experienced the internal mechanics of energy vibration. My psycho/physical being was like an electrical system being upgraded as I activated each energy center by concentrating on the vibrations there. Through my focused attention, the energy levels of my physical body rose in alignment with my Soul body, whose higher vibrations of peace and joy dissolved the lower, negative vibrations of grief and despair.

I would still have to deal with the natural trauma of Peter's death, but my life and my sense of self were irrevocably changed by this experience.

It proved to me that I am more than just a physical self. I am also an eternal being with extra-sensory powers of perception. And I knew intuitively that neither trauma and shock nor out-of-body experiences are required to achieve or activate the higher energy states of awareness I had experienced.

Recalling Peter's message that he was with Cupid and was surrounded by love, I knew that he was happy and wanted others to know he had gone to a good place. I didn't question the fact that Peter now existed in a non-physical world, in a dimension beyond the earth, as we all would someday.

I now understood the true meaning of Honey's message: "I am going to a good place where you, too, can go."

Those of us still physically alive can benefit here and now from the knowledge that there is no death; and that if we continue to exist in the hereafter, we can utilize the same energy mechanics deployed in my out-of-body-experience. We can raise our energy up into higher states of Soul consciousness to manage daily life from a more enlightened state—to transmute darkness into light.

The new understandings tied to the hexagonal ring had finally arrived!

As the unexpected blessings of my out-of-body experience gently mingled with my grief over Peter's death, finally, I fell fast asleep.

CHAPTER 15

Energy Hugs

Morning dawned outwardly tranquil and serene, but unbearable thoughts and emotions tormented me as I awoke to grapple with the agonizing reality of Peter's death. The bustling sounds coming from the kitchen afforded me some comfort.

Locked in grief, I wasn't ready to leave my room, to face others, to face a world without Peter. So, I chose not to.

I remained curled up in bed, looking out at the ruby-red bougainvillea that fanned across the guest room window, saved from utter despair by one unshakeable certainty. Peter's Soul, his higher self—his true self—was eternal. Peter was still alive!

I lay there grieving, craving Peter's presence. I longed to be with him again, if just for a moment, but was it possible?

I knew we had met the night before in a dimension unseen, but where was he now? I decided to call on him, Soul to Soul, to see if I could initiate contact. I took a moment to go within, closing my eyes, raising my energy, and visualizing Pete in my mind. Then I called out Peter's name as if beckoning him in from the backyard.

I attuned my Soul to Peter's, left the daily world behind, and went deeper within.

Soon I noticed familiar feelings and sensations. Goose bumps formed on my arms and chills ran up my spine. I sensed an electrical energy floating next to and somewhat above me. Peter's Soul body was in the room.

I did not see or hear him this time. I simply felt his spiritual presence—his electromagnetic field. I also experienced a kind of shock, caught off guard by the ease and intensity with which Peter had appeared. It was one thing to be involuntarily swept into another dimension through the gateway of severe shock and trauma. It was an entirely different matter to consciously call a disembodied Soul into the room.

I felt overwhelmed and my first impulse was to get up and run out into the kitchen to be with my family. Instead, I calmed my emotions and allowed myself to experience contact. Then my extrasensory mechanisms seemed to switch on.

I sensed waves of electrical currents emanating from Peter to me, drawing me towards him. I felt myself being spontaneously pulled up into his powerful aura like iron filings drawn to a magnet. My energy body melded into his invisible force field. Then we merged and embraced in a kind of energy hug, basking in the radiance of each other's magnetic presence. It was exquisitely serene and intimate. I could feel him feeling me, and it literally took my breath away.

This hug happened in an instant, but when it was gone, the serenity remained.

The phenomena I had experienced with Honey and Janet had been repeated with Peter. Only this time, I had consciously initiated it. The power of these hugs was extraordinary. It was so comforting, so uplifting, and I felt blessed to have experienced the tangible reality of the Soul's electromagnetic energy; both Peter's and mine.

Moments later I heard the distant ring of the telephone in the adjoining kitchen, followed by the words, "I'll see if she's up."

Fortunately, Peter's visitation had brought me comfort, and I was now ready and able to face the world. I felt a profound desire and determination to soldier on. I was willing to meet whatever the day, and my life, might bring.

All that day phone calls poured in from our devastated friends. I spoke with each and every caller, and my heart was warmed by the many people who said the exact same phrase, "He was my best friend." It was a testament not just to Peter's popularity, but to the largeness of his spirit and the many lives he had touched with his heart and Soul.

My morning contact with Peter and the extraordinary events the previous evening were a true blessing. They gave me an anchor to hold onto while friends from around the world shared their grief.

Initially, each caller seemed in shock, distraught and sorrowful, while I, Peter's grieving widow, was surprisingly calm and strong. I felt Peter's presence with me as his happiness and love moved through me like an uplifting current to touch all those who called. I felt angels by my side, strengthening and enfolding me as I delivered Pete's message of peace and comfort to our family and friends.

Over and over, I told each caller, "Peter came to me in a dream last night and said he is with Cupid, and he is surrounded by a lot of love."

As with Honey's messages, I spoke with conviction, and

immediately, I could hear a profound calmness returning to the sound of their voice.

I still wasn't comfortable discussing the full story, however. I didn't talk about the details of my out-of-body journey and my meetings with Peter and the Beings of light.

It was 1985, when near-death and out-of-body experiences were not commonly discussed. I knew my experiences would have been harder for people to accept if I told them as they had occurred, whereas they could easily relate to, and maybe find inspiration in them as a dream experience.

No doubt others might say that my experience was just a dream. Yet I knew that I had traveled into another dimension where messages had been telepathically transmitted to me both from Peter and from highly evolved beings of light. This had occurred in a waking state and had been one of the most profound experiences of my life.

Still, I found myself wondering at times if this experience had been real. It is always possible to doubt profoundly mystical and blessed experiences in a world that largely denies their reality.

This is where faith comes in.

I chose to believe in the reality and power of my experience rather than doubt and dismiss it with the skeptical mind of the world. The experience had changed and comforted me. It had given me renewed strength to deal with the crisis and the trauma of Peter's death, which would still take time to process and heal.

Throughout the morning and in between phone calls, I reflected on all the messages that had been communicated to me. I sat outside on the brick patio adjacent to the living room where the tree-lined canyon framed my parents' backyard. Relaxing my body, I focused my attention on the notes I had written down and relived the sequence of events.

One message in particular immediately stood out, "No matter how hard your lessons or how difficult life becomes, you have chosen to go into the earth plane and learn from your experiences."

This means that I chose to experience these tragedies from an early age in order, as they said, "to give your Soul the best opportunity to evolve."

The messages from the Beings of Light were so powerful, yet so foreign to me. Reading this really did bring me comfort, and at the same time left me wanting to understand more.

As I reflected on another message, "In one mortal lifetime, you will attempt to master at the most two or three challenging emotions," it made me wonder what my three challenging emotions were.

The first thing that came to mind was fear. Fear had been surrounding me for as long as I could remember. Identifying one emotion was good for the time being, so I went back inside and prepared to leave the house for Santa Monica.

Before staying at Dad and Jeanne's house, I had made another doctor's appointment. Now the doctor's appointment fell on the day after Peter's death.

My family said they would accompany me, so even in the midst of this tragedy I decided to keep the appointment. However, just as we were walking out the door, two distressing phone calls delayed our departure.

The first one was the mortuary calling to ask me if I wanted Peter embalmed.

"Embalmed," I asked, "what do you mean?"

"No, you don't need to!" Mom called out from across the room. "He's being cremated!"

As soon as I hung up, the coroner's office called.

Oddly, the coroner questioned me in-depth about Peter's friends—I didn't know at first that they were doing an investigation.

My parents finally interrupted and told me to tell the coroner that if they kept questioning me, we would need to get a lawyer. With that, the conversation ended, and I hung up the phone, puzzled by the exchange and the reason for the questions.

Then we left for the doctor's office.

A sense of sweet camaraderie prevailed as we walked into the clinic. After checking in, we sat together in an empty row of chairs at the back of the room, when another remarkable event occurred.

A woman sat down in the seat directly in front of me and opened a magazine. As I glanced over her shoulder, I saw a picture of Cupid displayed across a two-page spread. I grabbed Mom's arm as goose bumps spread over my body.

"Look, look," I blurted out, "it's Cupid!"

My family had heard my story that Peter was with Cupid many times, and the picture now struck a chord in all of us. To me particularly, it was an unmistakable indication of Peter's presence in the room. This was Peter's way of getting my attention, as if he were saying, "Hi, Lu!"

Aware of his presence near me, I took a moment to go within. Focusing on the now-familiar radiance of Peter's Soul body, I merged with him in an energy embrace, feeling again the sense of electromagnetic contact that seemed to be the signature of these inter-dimensional hugs.

Our hug filled me with a sense of peace, and fears about the status of my ear began to dissipate. Soon thereafter I was given the go-ahead to fly home.

Dad and Jeanne flew with me back to the Bay Area/Marin County. I was still suffering from my lingering ear infection, and the doctor had given me specific drugs to prevent damage to my eardrum.

As our plane took off into the morning sky, I suddenly recalled the words Peter had spoken to me right before we left for L.A., "Maybe I'm preparing you for when I die young. It won't be so hard on you."

Why did Peter say this? I wondered. Had he known? When Pete was 12 years old, he had come close to death after a fall from his grandmother's pool slide burst open his pancreas.

Was it then that Peter gained insight into his own Soul plan; a life blueprint stored deep in his subconscious all these years? Did his awareness come from the same source that had provided Janet with her information 12 years before it manifested? The similarity of these two events was remarkable, just like Ilana during the Munich Massacre, some form of subliminal preparation had occurred before his passing.

Chills ran through me as I became aware of the many life events that had prepared me for Peter's death. As he had prophesized many times over our 14-year relationship, he did die young, and the pain of our five days apart had prepared me for the ultimate separation.

Do loved ones always prepare us for their passing, although we are not aware of it?

One thing was for certain, Peter was now free. I saw how his Soul had entered the vibrations of the earth, temporarily embodied in a physical form known as Peter Peringer, and finally returned, wiser and richer through experience, to the eternal from whence he came.

These understandings further shifted my perceptions of Peter's death from the finality of an ending to the recognition of a new beginning.

CHAPTER 16

Enlightened Perspectives

After landing in San Francisco, Dad, Jeanne, and I drove 45 minutes across the Golden Gate Bridge to Marin County. Our first task was to meet Peter's family at the coroner's office in the Marin Civic Center.

When we arrived, the coroner sat us down and informed us that Pete had died from a heart attack that was under investigation. "A heart attack?" I questioned in shock.

No further details were given, and I simply signed the death certificate. When I asked the coroner for the clothes Peter was wearing the night he died, I was informed that they were at the mortuary where we would be purchasing his burial items.

The coroner then asked if we wanted to see Peter's body.

Without hesitation, I answered, "No."

I wanted my last image of Pete to be the morning Tam and I left for Los Angeles, not the empty shell of the body he had left behind.

The drive to the mortuary was a blur. I was anticipating just one thing—seeing Peter's clothes from the night he died and feeling closer to the person I so dearly loved.

It didn't take long to pick out Peter's urn. After finalizing all the arrangements, I nervously asked the mortician if I could have Pete's clothes. He left the room to get them, and I waited anxiously for him to return. My heart was pounding.

Finally, the mortician reappeared and silently handed me a large brown paper bag. My hands were trembling as I opened it to peer inside.

I could not believe what I saw.

The outfit Pete was wearing when he died was his grey corduroy pants and white "Jazzercise" t-shirt—the outfit I had laid out for him while he showered the morning we left for L.A.

I quickly walked outside and burst into tearful laughter. While cradling Pete's last outfit in my arms, I felt his unmistakable presence.

The details of Peter's cremation were completed, and plans were in place to bury his ashes at the Peringer family plot in Washington State. We also planned for a celebration of life to be held later the following week.

One of the hardest tasks of all was still before me. It was time to pick Tamarin up from school and tell her the news—her Papa was gone.

As the bell rang, Tam's second grade classroom door flew open and immediately she saw me, Dad, and Jeanne. The smile on her face was comforting as she jumped into my arms and gave us all a great big hug.

The two-block ride to our house seemed like an eternity, but once at home we sat alone on the living room floor and I cautiously told her, "Tam, I have some sad news to tell you."

Pausing for a moment I continued, "Peter has passed away, sweetie. The doctors tell us he had a heart attack early yesterday morning."

I saw the intent look on her face turn to confusion as her big beautiful blue eyes squinted in pain.

I continued, "Papa's has gone on to heaven, Tam, and even though he can't be here in the house with us any longer, he can be our angel watching over and protecting us."

Tamarin was silent. She didn't say a word, internalizing the horrifying moment. So, I held her and asked, "Do you have any questions? Is there anything you want to ask me, anything at all?"

Tamarin looked up at me and said, "Mommy, does this mean that you are going to die too?"

I looked her straight in the eyes and lovingly said, "No sweetie, don't you worry. I will be here with you for a long, long time. If you are ever worried about that or have any other questions about Peter, please let me know. Okay? Promise?"

Tears welled up in her eyes and then Tamarin replied while crying, "Okay, I promise."

Next, I contacted Pete's teachers and loved ones in India. It was March, and the end of the winter concert season. Zakir and Alla Rakha were in Mumbai on their yearly performance tour, and Zakir's wife, Toni, was there on a grant to study Kathak dance with her guru Sitara Devi. Peter's close friend Geoffrey was in Kolkata studying with the masters there.

I composed short telegrams to both Mumbai and Kolkata, letting everyone know that our dear friend Peter had passed.

With these tasks now completed, Dad and Jeanne took an early morning flight back to L.A., leaving a void that was quickly filled.

Thankfully, Pete's sister, Jennifer, came to stay at the condo. For the next few nights, friends gathered at our home for late-night vigils talking, laughing, and crying in memory of Pete.

These powerful gatherings were spontaneously organized and were a source of great healing for all of us.

Soon, however, Jennifer went home.

In the days that followed I watched myself careen between hell and heaven.

On the one hand, I was haunted by a nagging sense that I could have done more to keep Peter on this earth, sharing his God-given musical talent with the world and the people who loved him.

On the other hand, amongst the grief and sorrow these thoughts generated, an awareness of deeper truths slowly began to solidify as I strived to maintain new insights and understandings—to feel peace.

I reflected on the place of Soul consciousness, on the concepts I now understood to be undeniable truths. Yes, the Soul body we will become upon the death of our physical body is within us now. When we access it, we can receive the strength needed to maintain enlightened perspectives for every challenge that comes into our lives, even the most tragic.

As a result, we grow and evolve!

Thankfully too, flowers, letters, and phone calls continually arrived at our house, making this tragic event even more bearable.

One phone call in particular was incredibly special. Zakir had received my telegram and called from Mumbai to send his condolences. His first question to me was, "How are you doing?"

Once again, I felt blessed to have Peter's messages to impart, but this time I told Zakir the true story.

"Peter visited with me the night he died and said that he was surrounded by love," I replied matter-of-factly.

This was the first time that I had openly told anyone, other than family, about Peter's after-death communication—it wasn't just a dream. Telling Zakir the truth was natural and spontaneous, as I instinctively knew he would understand.

We shared our grief, and I was grateful for the love and compassion Zakir sent my way.

Next came Pete's celebration of life. We held it in our Condo complex at the home of our close friend, Jimmy. It was a wonderful gathering that brought together family, many close friends, and students from the college.

Pete's tabla drums were prominently displayed in the living room around a beautiful picture of him sitting in a chair, smiling happily while drumming on his legs. This photo of Pete filled the room with the essence of his love and devotion. Two candles were lit on either side of the display, and the flowers people brought contributed significantly to our sacred altar.

Then, a few days after the celebration, I received shocking news.

The coroner's initial report had stated that Peter had died of a heart attack. He had complained for weeks about numbness in his left arm and even received acupuncture treatments for it. We had thought that the problem was a result of practicing for long hours on a new type of drum. When I also reflected on how Pete had felt faint in the bathroom at Pam's house, all these events did paint a picture of a weak heart.

Now, 10 days later, the coroner's final report arrived. It documented that Peter's heart attack was caused by a cocaine overdose.

This was surprising news. Doing coke had not been a part of Pete's life for many years. With the report, rumors started flying. People speculated that Peter had been murdered with an intentionally administered overdose of crack cocaine; that he had committed suicide by ingesting a bag of coke; or, that he did have a weak heart and simply didn't have the same tolerance as when he was younger.

For myself, I had to accept that I would never know what had happened the night Pete passed on. Eventually, it really didn't matter. I simply rode the waves of grief, pain, and worry as they passed through me. I released them as best I could, accepting Peter's passing as an event beyond my control.

To me, Peter's life had passed in the blink of an eye, like a meteorite blazing across the sky. Part of my grief was in my wondering...had he done all that he came here to do?

So, I asked myself...was I accomplishing all that I came here to do? How would I know?

Having activated my Soul body during my out-of-body experience (OBE), I now had a tangible feeling for this immaterial entity known as the Soul. That accomplishment was surely going to make it easier for me to build not only a strong mind and body, but to also incorporate the Soul into my life and build its enlightened perspectives as my primary reality.

Bottom line, life is short. I needed to ensure that my fleeting embodiment on this earth was as productive as possible.

As I watched the morning sun rise above the hills of Marin County, its gentle radiance filled me with a sense of calm and contentment from which I drew strength. My outlook on life and death had changed forever. It felt like I was experiencing everything for the first time from a clear perspective, like a newborn child.

Yes, I had tapped into a power in the universe beyond human imagining that I yearned to know more about with every fiber of my being. I had gained insights guiding me to fulfill my higher purpose and my reason for being.

Yet, I also knew that my personality with its thoughts and emotions of pain and grief still lay beneath this present calm.

At any moment, my personality could rise painfully within me, paralyzing me, consuming my mind, my peace, and my very being. It could easily call me into the darkness, tormenting me with thoughts that my life will never be the same without Pete.

Even with new insights, something in me still followed my personality into the darkness and the pain. So, I let myself ride the wave of grief and sorrow when it came.

Knowing, however, that life is short, I also shifted in those moments and practiced holding the enlightened perspective of joy.

I knew that holding joy would take time, but I did practice joyful thinking whenever I could. I felt joyful that Tamarin and I had each other. I felt the joy of hugging her, cooking for her, and spotting her frequent handstands and cartwheels.

Often Tam would ask me where Papa went, and if she could see him. I would try to stay strong, find a sense of joy, and explain as best I could. "Papa is still with us, Tam, but he's now living in his Soul body. When you go to sleep at night you can be with him and see him in your dreams."

Tamarin's awareness and insight astounded me. She often held Peter's urn in her lap and hugged it with all her might. As she did this one night, she looked up at me and said, "Mommy, I know Papa isn't in here. He's with me. I can talk to him if I need to."

Another evening, I walked past Tamarin's room after she had gone to bed. She slept with her door open, so I looked in.

Tam was sitting upright in her pinewood four-post bed,

leaning against a heart-shape carved into the headboard. Her long blonde, disheveled hair was strewn over her flannel nightgown, and her large blue eyes were wide open. Tam was looking up to her right. She didn't seem to be awake, or at least not in normal waking consciousness.

Just then she raised her arm, shook her finger in the air, and in a sweet motherly tone, said, "Papa, I want you to know that we love you very much, now you go and do good."

She reached out both arms as if for a hug. Then she lay down and went to sleep. When I asked her about it the next morning, Tam didn't have any memory of the experience.

I knew that Tam was also in contact with Peter.

CHAPTER 17

Doorway to the Soul

A month had passed since Peter's death. As I lay in my room, the morning sun, now in full view, stained the clouds with an orange glow as the birds chirped noisily while flitting from tree to tree. A ray of sunlight cascaded through the window touching down upon the wine-colored bookshelf leaning against my wall.

Nature's spotlight drew my attention to the top shelf, pointing to a book resting sideways. The title was, *The Dream Book* by Betty Bethards.

Suddenly, the memory of one of my dreams flashed into my mind, producing a kind of shock within me.

"Oh, my God. My dream!" I said to myself.

I threw back the covers, went to the closet and pulled out the dream journal I had brought with me to L.A. just before Peter's death. I opened it, and there on the first page was a dream I had forgotten until just now:

DREAM NOTATION March 1, 1985

I was in the house that I grew up in on Las Palmas. I was in Debby's room, but I was with another guy and not Peter. I felt close to this guy. Courtney (my childhood buddy) came in and I was glad to see him because I was confused why I wasn't with Peter. Courtney very calmly explained, "Everything is going to be all right Mama (my college nickname)—everything is going to be all right. This was the way your life was meant to go." He nodded sincerely and said, "You will understand more later. It's going to be all right."

DREAM NOTATION March 1, 1985

Immediately following my recorded dream was a notation which I had written soon after. It read:

I called our high school buddy, Jay, this morning to say hi. I asked if he had heard from Courtney lately and he said, "Yes, he just called me last night." That was the same night of my dream—weird! I am scared from this dream because I don't want to be with another person. I want to be with Peter. I am confused why I was with another guy? Why was Courtney saying that everything was going to be all right? What was going to be all right? Was something going to happen?

The shock of Peter's death had overwhelmed me. I had completely forgotten about this dream until now. Peter had died the night I had it, and Courtney had come into my dream to subtly warn me of the impending change.

Had this dream subconsciously prepared me for Peter's passing, and what forces operating within the dream would come, prophetically, to prepare me for events that had not yet occurred?

The prophetic nature of my dream with Courtney confirmed for me that, yes, there was a plan in operation greater than any I could comprehend or over-ride. If this was the way my life was meant to go, as Courtney had said, then it must be the way Peter's life was meant to go. His Soul was on a mission, following a plan that was not mine to control. He had fulfilled his Soul's plan. His death was accomplished fate. There was no need for me to worry.

But why did I, or anyone, experience fear, doubt, pain, insecurity, anger, frustration, and other difficult feelings?

Then I reflected once again on the messages from the Beings of Light. I knew with certainty that not only do loved ones never die, but they also live according to a predetermined Soul plan. This meant that I, too, was living according to an unfolding plan that existed beyond my conscious knowledge or comprehension. Yet I still didn't know what my Soul plan contained.

Realizing that more answers were sure to come, I watched the lives of those around me return to normal and continue as if nothing had happened. But mine was changed forever.

The coroner's office had sent me a letter asking if I wanted grief counseling. But something inside me instinctively knew what had to be done. I was in a process that was going to be anything but brief. It was like finding myself in the middle of the ocean, riding waves to a distant shore. It would take however long it took.

In those first weeks my tears came every few hours. They were strong. And I'd cry suddenly, at a thought, at a sound. But as time went on, my crying spells subsided, which signaled healing. I would cry every other day, then a few times a week. Eventually, these crying spells came infrequently, but they always took me by complete surprise.

I'd be driving in my car or walking in the market, and suddenly I'd burst into tears. I never knew when it would happen. I decided not to resist. When it came, I just let myself sob, releasing the pain that needed to burst out of me. I allowed myself to grieve, to feel and release whatever emotions and feelings arose in me rather than allowing them to eat me alive.

The shock and grief of Peter's death also triggered bouts of insomnia, which diminished my prolific dream life. But after recalling my prophetic dream from the night of Peter's death, I began to wonder, "If my dreams could provide prophetic council, what else could they bestow?"

I didn't know but was ready to find out, so I kept my journal by the bed. I looked expectantly to my dreams as one looks to a teacher, hoping for dream revelations that would answer the questions and mysteries that now consumed my life.

Gradually, my insomnia diminished, and I attempted to log as many of my dreams as possible. Initially, I couldn't remember most of them. I'd dream of Peter often, but when I awoke and tried to remember these dreams, they were disjointed and elusive. The harder I tried to recall them, the more they tended to recede from my awareness, often disappearing without a trace.

Determined to recapture my dream life, I created a three-step dream request plan, and set out to make it work. The basic format was simple:

1) Identify the intent.
2) Visualize the results.
3) Affirm the outcome.

It went as follows:

Step 1: In this step I expressed my intent verbally, either aloud or silently to myself. I used the words, "I will meet up with Peter in my dreams, learn more about my Soul plan, and remember everything."

This set my intent in motion, which was to be with him if even for a fleeting moment, to see his smile, hold his hand, or look him in the eyes; and to learn more about why I am here.

I knew now that it wasn't necessary to be psychic or have extraordinary powers to obtain these desired results. The intent was all that was needed to trigger the dreams, and my recall.

It was much like praying for help in a crisis, or for insights into a dilemma. Somehow, it invoked a response from that mysterious power greater than me. My operating principle reflected the words of Jesus, "Ask and ye shall receive."

Step 2: Once my intent was clearly expressed, I anchored it by seeing with my inner eye. Using my imagination and the power of visualization, I held in my mind an image of Peter communicating to me, and then waking up and recalling an impactful dream. Doing this focused and magnified my intent. It was much like tuning a radio to a specific station until I could hear the music clearly.

Step 3: Next, the process had to be finalized. To do this I affirmed with all my might, "I am having a dream in which all I need to know is given forth."

This statement declared the goal in its complete form, gave the command to make it happen, and sent signals to dissolve any thoughts and emotions that might block the desired results. Using this affirmation just before falling asleep was a powerful stage in the process that made its manifestation certain.

I usually went to sleep with a clear picture of Peter firmly planted in my mind. In the beginning I wasn't sure what the results would be. I soon discovered that the power of the mind, when joined with the will with a clearly conceived intent, caused amazing things to happen.

I kept a cassette tape recorder, and my journal, by the bedside each night. The following are some of my dreams that came as a result, followed by the dreams notations I logged afterwards.

DREAM NOTATION April 19, 1985

I was driving in a car down Sir Francis Drake Blvd past our condominium complex. A friend was driving me, and I looked back out the window and saw Peter sitting on a bench in front of the condos. I held my hand out the window, and as we waved to each other Peter yelled out, "Hey, I'll wait here for you."

DREAM NOTATION April 19, 1985

I awakened from this dream sobbing. It felt so real, as if we had actually been together and the reality upon awakening of me here while Peter was still there hit me hard. I remember so clearly looking back at Pete waving goodbye—reaching out for him, and then feeling myself slide back into my body. Was I with him while I slept?

I know this is also a message. I must go on with my life,

but I will return to him one day and he will be waiting for me on the other side. There is no time or space as we know it in the dimensional reality of the Soul state.

I remembered the feeling of sliding back into my physical body after this dream! At that moment of re-entry, I recognized the subtle essence of my Soul as easily as I could my body into which it had entered. Before re-entry, my awareness seemed to exist somewhere between the denser physical state and the superior Soul state.

During sleep I was released from physical limitations as my body slept—my consciousness merged with my Soul body. It was the same feeling evoked the night Peter died, when an electromagnetic energy filled my room, shifting me into a higher dimension.

I soon realized that dreams are the doorway to the Soul. Dreams verify that the Soul is not limited by time, space, or even by death. They demonstrate that while the body sleeps, our Soul accesses other realities and dimensions. There, we can have life-altering experiences and receive life-changing information.

In the dream-state, we can meet with departed loved ones, celestial beings, and the Souls of the living. In our dreams, it is possible to visit, play, communicate, work, and even continue to grow together with the Souls of departed loved ones who, I am convinced, remain for a time in a dimension close to the earth upon passing away. My dreams showed me how thin the veil is between these two worlds.

It was different from my out-of-body experience because, this time, I was not in normal waking consciousness. I was awake in another realm while my body slept on the bed. When my dream ended, the experience of separating from Peter once again and the tantalizing closeness of these two worlds were more than I could bear. I could not help bursting into tears.

My dream plan had worked. Peter's words, "I'll wait here for you," were also immensely comforting. They helped me know that when I do leave my physical body and this world behind, Peter would be waiting for me on the other side. I knew Honey and Janet would be waiting as well.

My dreams began increasing in numbers, length, and content. Eventually, they filled my entire journal.

Pete and I were continuing our relationship in the dream-state. My nightly visits with Peter in my Soul body not only convinced me that dreams occurred in a zone of reality we shared with those who had died, but also offered another explanation for Honey's message, "I am going to a good place where you, too, can go."

I felt so grateful that answers to lifelong questions continued to come forth.

DREAM NOTATION May 16, 1985

I drove up the driveway to a friend's house and Peter was standing by the front door. He was dressed in all white and we stopped to talk. He said he wasn't going to hang out long because there was no point since he couldn't materialize. We started talking about the fact that I was asleep and out of my body. It was time for me to go back and he couldn't. He was not able to materialize, and I realized he was feeling remorseful about the fact that everyone was on the earth plane, and he wasn't.

So, I told him, "This is what I see of what we are experiencing. This is how our life is meant to be. You're here now, there's nothing we can do about it, but it is such a beautiful thing. I helped you to the point before your death and you are helping me in your death. I am trying really hard to accept our new relationship. Please, I know my thoughts and sadness have affected you and I am sorry for that. Maybe as I can grow from my grief, we can both accept it and see what a beautiful feeling we are having now, in this new way. It's not what we had planned, but it is good."

I asked if he liked the spiritual experiences, and he completely lit up and said, "Yes, so much," and he hugged me. Then Peter continued by saying, "You must love you and know you and feel secure in who you are and my love for you beyond a body, but as a Soul. If you knew this, your grief could subside, and I could more easily move on. By showing you this it can develop into a knowing for you, so you can use your doubt, fear, and insecurity as opportunities to learn and grow."

We hugged again and I said, "thank you." We both knew this was now our new relationship.

DREAM NOTATION May 16, 1985

Peter not only told me he was now there to love me as a Soul, but he also encouraged me to let my grief begin to subside. Was my sorrow actually a concern for him? I had even apologized in my dream for my sadness. Once I thought for a moment it made sense—yes, it was. As with any physical relationship, it was painful to see loved ones suffer. In his new life, Peter worried about me healing from his passing on.

In this dream, it appeared that Peter had to suddenly deal with the fact that he could no longer return with me into the physical realm. Peter was experiencing a period of cross-over adjustment, feeling bad and remorseful that he couldn't return to accomplish more in this life.

What Peter had accomplished while on earth was now set in stone. There was no going back, no changing anything that had transpired, no more accelerated growth through human experiences and relationships. He was done here and must adjust to that fact. It was time for him to move on.

That dream taught me that the departed also grieve. I knew I must let my grief subside so that Peter could move on and not be painfully tied by me to a world he could no longer enjoy. It seemed that my dreams were teaching and guiding me, giving me answers. They revealed their higher purpose by showing me how to meet and move through the problems I faced in my waking life.

Amazingly, our Souls were still talking through frustrations and fears, only this time inter-dimensionally. We gave each other advice, and Peter's words, "You must love you and know you and feel secure in who you are," were just what I needed to move forward in my life.

I recalled the night Peter died, how I had prayed for him to be taken to the highest place possible, and how, in a dream, he told me, "Your prayers have moved me on." So, I knew it was also important to pray for his spiritual transition into his new life.

All of this made me wonder again about the status of my own sojourn here on earth. Was I accomplishing my Soul's plan? If I died tomorrow, would I feel unfulfilled and full of regrets?

I wanted to look back after death and know that I had accomplished my mission on earth. My mission still remained somewhat mysterious to me, but my dreams now seemed to hold keys to solving such mysteries. And they provided some consolation for my loss of Peter in this life.

Yet the ability to see and feel Peter in the Soul-state in my dreams didn't replace the conversations, the camaraderie, or the sound of his laughter. The pain of Peter's passing was still very intense. My fears and doubts had trapped me, held me back, and stopped me from exercising the inner power of my Soul. And it was time to let them go.

CHAPTER 18

Soul Fitness Program

My dream conversations with Peter often gave me a new focus and a sense of hope in my waking life. Peter's words, "You can use your fear and insecurity to learn and grow," pointed to answers regarding my Soul plan.

My fear and insecurity were calling me to observe myself in daily life. They were a spiritual challenge and an opportunity to practice recognizing and transforming the painful limitations of my human personality. These feelings were urging me to simply choose who I wanted to be in the face of these difficulties, as the Beings of Light had said. But how do I consistently make that happen?

Then it dawned on me.

If I could create a plan to invoke spiritual dreams and connect with my Soul, virtually at will, then surely, I could create a plan to maintain my Soul's wisdom, strength, and guidance in the waking state.

Also, if I could hear the after-death presence, the eternal Soul, of my loved ones, then I could certainly learn to consistently tune in and strengthen the voice of my own Soul while in my body.

So, I adapted my three-step Dream Request Plan into a Soul Fitness Program to practice strengthening my Soul's enlightened perspectives and change the way I perceived and responded to events in my daily life: 1) Identify the intent. 2) Visualize the results. 3) Affirm the outcome.

As I recalled my words to Peter in my dream, "This is how our lives were meant to go," I also recognized them as the same words Courtney had spoken to me in an earlier prophetic dream.

In these words, I practiced identifying the voice of my Soul speaking above the doubt and fear that bound my human personality in the waking world. In my Soul, I knew it was not up to me to prevent Peter's death. That was the truth I needed to anchor in my mind in my waking life.

So, I visualized Peter's life completed perfectly as planned. Practicing this transformed my fear once again into a sense of trust in a higher plan and the feeling that Pete had accomplished his goals.

To solidify this new perspective and prevent worry and fear from seizing control, I affirmed to myself, and Peter, "I am content with the time we spent together and joyful for your transition."

I now knew that if I disciplined myself to implement my own Soul Fitness Program—to listen within, to hear the voice of my Soul, and visualize and affirm its perspective as my reality—then I could consistently transform fear, insecurity, or any other negative emotion that afflicted my personality.

More importantly I could build the strength of my eternal self and live in a happier, wiser, and higher state of being a greater percentage of time. This is how, as the Beings of Light had said, I would choose who I wanted to be in the face of difficulties!

Eventually, with practice, this inner voice would communicate to me more and more, both in my dreams and discretely in my daily life.

DREAM June 7, 1985

We were at a house with a group of friends and Peter was sitting on the counter with his leather jacket on. All of a sudden, Peter walked over to give a speech to everyone about how he didn't really die, and that the coroners had brought him back to life by working on him. I couldn't believe he was not dead. I kept saying, "But they told me you were dead."

And Peter kept saying in reply, "Well they were wrong." He went on to say that he has a plan now. "There is so much ahead for us to all share, and I am really looking forward to it. I am ready for my new life. I went to school and talked to the teachers today and they signed me up with a whole program so I can study my weaknesses and learn to develop self-confidence and self-esteem to become successful.

There is a lot of life left ahead and hopefully everyone can learn something from what I have to share. God bless you and God bless me and God bless all of us in our new life together." He walked over and smiled and toasted his glass of wine to mine and then Peter went and sat down.

Everyone was stunned, the room was quiet, and no one moved. I knew that there was a lot of work ahead, but Peter was growing, we were all growing, driven by the power of love. I was so high, a good balanced high, excited that Peter was still alive!

When I awoke from this dream, I thought that Peter was still alive and then had to go through the realization that it was only a dream—only a dream that he was not dead!

Usually, we awaken from bad dreams happy to realize that it was only a dream. This time I awoke from a good dream sad to realize that it was only a dream.

Peter said he was not dead. He wanted everyone to know he really was alive, and he had a plan. He was in school studying his weaknesses. Peter said in many of my dreams that he was alive and in school, and that he had so much to learn, to grow, and to share. His repeated messages merged with messages from the Beings of Light and accelerated the transformation within me.

It became clear to me that I am in the school of life—to learn, to grow, and to share. The success Peter spoke of in my dream was not about money, fame, or fancy cars. It was about following our plan to develop mastery over weaknesses such as anger, insecurity, and doubt.

Yes, we design demanding situations that generate specific emotions—two or three as the Beings of Light had said—that give us the opportunities to grow. That was the true meaning of success and further confirmed the answer to what our higher purpose is in this lifetime!

If I identify which specific emotions I have come here to master, then I have reverse engineered my Soul plan—I have reproduced through detailed examination exactly what I planned to experience in this lifetime.

I knew that as long as I implemented my Soul Fitness Program, I would move forward on my life path and the full contents of my Soul plan would eventually be revealed.

As Peter moved on in the next dimension, my dreams tapered

off. The transformations in him, and his adjustment to life after death, were apparent in my dream progressions. In a later dream, Peter appeared very angelic radiating a big smile across the room. Everyone was asking him what it was like to be dead and how it felt to him. Peter smiled and told them what a wonderful experience it was. He said, "Here where I am now, this is reality—where you are, it is temporary."

In the light of this clarity, my chronic sense of isolation, caused by my unusual experiences, began to diminish. My Soul Fitness Program became a daily practice and evolved into a distinct process to transform my fear and insecurity into trust and confidence—to use thoughts and emotions as a means to transform the challenges of daily life into an enlightened state of Soul consciousness.

As a result, I became increasing aware of how much I had to share with others, and it was time to put all that was inside me out on the table. I knew it was time to talk openly about my after-death communications, to feel confident in what I had learned, and then let the doubters doubt.

First, however, it was time to bury Peter's ashes.

On a bitterly cold May afternoon I drove with Peter's family—the Peringers—from Spokane to a quaint, tree-lined cemetery just outside Oaksdale, Washington. Oaksdale, a small town owned and operated by generations of Peringers, is the burial site of the Peringer clan dating back to 1856.

Three months had passed since Peter's death. His tombstone was ready. All the necessary burial arrangements were in place, and it was time to lay his ashes to rest.

Upon arriving, we were greeted by the cemetery director and escorted to the top of a grassy hill overlooking the rolling countryside. The sky was clear and sunny, but an icy wind cut through our coats and penetrated to the bone. Huddling together, we walked along a narrow pathway to the Peringer family headstone that marked the site where generations of Peter's family lay together.

Peter's grave site was next to the tombstone of his father, Roy P. Peringer, dated 1924–1977. We gathered in a tight semicircle around both of their graves. Six of us clutching one another, pressed together for warmth and consolation while listening to the minister deliver the service. As he spoke, I silently asked Peter for a sign if he was present. Would he come to his own burial?

The ceremony was short but emotional. Near the end, the minister lifted Pete's urn to the sky, and then bent to lower it into the earth. We all watched, intent and silent, each in our own way paying respects to a Soul who would be sorely missed.

Suddenly, the moment Peter's urn entered the grave, a sonic boom exploded in the sky and shook the earth beneath our feet. It was the most powerful sonic boom I had ever heard.

"Pete was that you?" I spoke to him silently.

Given my otherworldly contacts with Peter since his death, this uncanny event was to me a sign that his after-death presence was with us in spirit form. The sonic boom sounded just as his ashes were laid in the earth. Peter, a drummer with a flair for the dramatic, had indeed gone out with a bang!

"How did that happen?" I wondered.

Could Peter's spirit coordinate the speed of a plane flying over his burial at the precise moment his urn was laid in his grave? There are many stories of after-death presence in every age and culture; clocks and watches stop; lights turn inexplicably on or off; objects move, break, or fall, appear, or disappear; strange

181

images appear on windows or in photographs; large birds fly by; and there may be weather phenomena like rainbows or flashes of lightning.

For me, Peter's sonic boom was a perfectly apt sign by which he communicated his Soul's presence.

Now letting go of one another, we were each given the shovel to cover a bit of dirt over his urn. With the last shovelful of earth laid over his urn and his grave covered by a small mound of dirt; the service concluded. We stood in silence, paying our last respects. Then we walked away.

Peter's funeral brought closure and a sense of finality to my process of letting go. That felt very liberating. Most importantly, with a Soul Fitness Program in my toolbox, I was set to get to work and practice.

However, my financial situation had become more pressing with every passing week. I knew it was time to go back to full-time work. I needed a new career and a new life. With Peter gone, working from home was no longer an option. It was time to get back into the work world.

PART 5
HERE
TO
EVOLVE

CHAPTER 19

Meditation Moments

It was now the year 2000, and magic was in the air. Higher truths by which we might lead better lives were coming through many spiritual leaders and extra-dimensional stories began to enter the mainstream. Workshops and spiritual retreats were regularly being offered and metaphysical bookstores were opening all over the country.

I had built a full-time career in the software industry while putting pen to paper and drafting my story. It had also been nearly 15 years since Peter passed, and Tam was now 22 years old. After dedicating nearly two decades to my career and the gift of motherhood, it was time to find a new relationship.

That's when I met Rob and his two daughters, Nikole and Kelli.

Rob had separated from his wife of 25 years and had been living for six months in the apartment beneath his childhood friend's house. It was Cinco de Mayo and time for our annual party, where it was my tradition to fry tortilla chips and make my mom's famous guacamole.

Rob's oldest daughter, Nikole, lovingly known as Nik, was a senior in high school and dating the youngest son of the family hosting our party. Nik had gone to visit her dad a few days prior and adamantly told him, "You need to get out of the house and come to this party. You can meet new people!"

Rob honored her wishes and was the new guy at the party.

At one point during the evening, I looked over and noticed that Rob wasn't drinking. Immediately I approached him and asked, "Where's your cocktail?"

He quickly replied, "I don't drink. I'm diabetic."

That moment changed both our lives forever.

Tamarin had been diagnosed as diabetic at 13 years old, and she was now struggling with the disease. Rob's diabetic announcement was the opening we needed to dive into wonderful and informative conversations, talking at length on matters that were deeply pertinent to us both.

We have been together ever since.

Kelli was 13 years old at the time, and I have been her stepmother for more than half her life. When Kelli gave birth to her son, Geo, I also became Grammy, just like my mom!

I am so grateful that Rob, Nik, and Kelli entered my life, and for the special bond we have to this day. Yes, I am with another guy, and this is the way my life was meant to go as Courtney had so prophetically said in my dream so many years ago.

At the same time, there was still a void in my life. I desperately wanted to meet and engage in conversation with someone, anyone, who had witnessed an after-death presence and could collaborate with me on our experiences. I still felt so alone in this regard and decided to pray for companionship.

On a break from writing one Saturday afternoon, I sat in my

back yard to go within and consciously ask for what I needed. Shafts of sunlight filtered through the trees, shining on the hummingbirds hovering around their feeder. I took a long slow deep breath, and closing my eyes to the outside world, I relaxed and entered the place of power within. Then I fervently prayed to God, to my own Soul, and all spiritual forces that guided me.

"Please, lead me to someone who can give me confirmation and comfort in my journey to discuss the true nature of the Soul and share that knowledge with others."

I repeated this several times and sat quietly for a few minutes, feeling the peace within. Then, knowing that answers to prayer aren't always immediate, I got up, turned my attention to more practical matters, and went about my day.

Eager to begin a new project at work, I took a trip to the local bookstore. What had started as pioneering work in the field of database programming at the San Francisco Ballet had now become a director position in software development, and I wanted to buy the latest books on computer technology.

After finding what I needed, the metaphysical section called me over. Always eager to find a new spiritual book, I voraciously scanned the shelves for something to catch my eye.

Immediately, I was drawn to a small white book titled, *There is no Death* by Betty Bethards.

"What?" I exclaimed quietly to myself. "Betty Bethards!"

I had met Betty thirty years prior to this after reading her book *Atlantis*. Its spiritual concepts were so enlightening for me that I had called her publisher, Inner Light Foundation, to find her. To my surprise, not only was Betty's publisher her own company, but also it was located just 20 minutes away in the town of Novato where she booked private readings.

In the years since, I had met with Betty several times when I needed help with difficult periods in my life. Peter had even gone to speak with her about the mood swings that plagued him. Now, with her book, *There is No Death*, resting in the palm of my hand, I knew it was time to pay Betty another visit.

This was the answer to my prayers! Betty was exactly the person I had prayed to connect with.

While standing in line at the cashier, I glanced over the chapter titles and read the dedication to Betty's two sons. Sadly, both had died tragically young. I went straight home and insatiably devoured every chapter. The contents were utterly astounding. Betty's perspectives on life and death mirrored my own experiences.

As soon as I finished reading, I called and made an appointment to see her.

Betty had become a popular Bay Area mystic and lecturer as well as a prolific author. She was also well known through her radio and television appearances in the United States and Canada and had earned the respectful title of "The Commonsense Guru."

I was eager to see Betty again, however, this time, our visit would be different. Rather than having the usual reading from Betty, I was going to interview her!

When I arrived, Betty greeted me at the door with loving open arms. Her reddish-brown hair was perfectly coifed around her beautifully sculptured face. Now 66 years old, Betty's smile lit up the room, making her appear ageless. We had always had a close connection and were excited to see each other again.

Betty led me into her office, and we sat down next to one another. She took a quick sip from her Pepsi and leaned back in her favorite comfortable chair.

Without hesitation Betty asked, "So, what can I do for you today?"

I paused for a moment, realizing she didn't know about Peter's passing. Surprisingly, a wave of emotion welled up in me. My eyes began to tear up a bit as I told her,

"Well, Betty, Peter died in March 1985."

Betty gasped. "Oh, honey, I am so sorry. He seemed like he was doing so well the last time he was here. How are you doing?"

"Well, that's why I am here," I said.

She looked at me lovingly and asked again, "What can I do for you?"

I paused to gather my thoughts. My heart was pounding.

"The night of Peter's passing I had an out-of-body experience and was given messages by Beings of Light," I began. "Since then, Peter has come to me in so many ways to show that there truly is no death,"

"The same thing had happened years ago," I continued. "My grandmother and grandfather both visited me after they had died. These experiences have been really comforting, but they have also been totally isolating for me."

I didn't need to say anything more. Betty nodded in recognition.

"It sounds like you've had quite a few awakenings for someone so young," she said. "That's really good. Usually, it doesn't happen until later in life."

"Awakenings, what do you mean?" I asked.

"My biggest awakening was my own near-death experience," Betty replied. "That turned my world around. I had had experiences before that, but I never understood anything until my own death. Then I realized—Oh my God, there is no death!"

"When you realize this," Betty continued, "it changes your whole

189

perception of reality. You have to stop and ask, 'What is life and why am I here?'"

Betty got quiet for a moment. She was somewhere else. Then she sat upright in her chair and earnestly said, "I believe we must earn the right to die, and that it's a privilege to die. I don't believe in accidents where death is concerned."

"How do we earn the right? By coming here with a plan?" I asked reiterating the truths now felt deeply within me. "By doing what we set out to do and fulfilling our Soul plan?"

"Yep. Hopefully, we try our best and get it done before we leave. There is no death. We're here to learn and evolve. I want to get it right and finish it now, so I don't have to come back and try again."

I thought about my own desire to find and fulfill my Soul plan. I felt a wave of blessings envelope me as Betty showered me with these enlightened confirmations.

"When your sons' died, did they come to you?" I asked.

"Yeah! They came in spirit. And as a voice," she said. "I had a dream before Chris died, on April 9th in the middle of the night. In my dream I saw the death calendar of another woman who had died in the month of March. Then I saw this cute little fat clock with arms and legs and a little ball on its head running down the path going to the right. A voice said, 'Time is running out.' I woke up around 3:12 a.m. and wrote down 'death calendar, time is running out.'"

"Then the doorbell rang. Before I went to the front door, I knew Chris was dead. I said to myself, 'Oh my God, Chris is dead.' I knew. I knew what it was, and I didn't want to go to the door. I said to myself, 'Got to go to the door, I don't want to go to the door.'"

"So, I went to the door, and I opened it. It was the police, and I said, 'Chris?'"

"Then right away, I asked, 'he's killed?'"

"They confirmed that yes, he had died."

"Chris was killed riding his motorcycle on the road approaching the Golden Gate Bridge. Somehow, I knew. It was as if my guidance gave me the dream to say, 'Be prepared, kid.' They had to be coming up my driveway when I had the dream. It was just two minutes notice. I felt like God was saying, 'Okay honey, you know there's no death. Hang in there. There's nothing you can do.' Afterwards, I thought, 'Well, God loved me enough to give me that.'"

Betty continued, "Then I went into the kitchen to call the coroner in San Francisco. In my mind I was fussing at Chris about the motorcycle. Right then I heard him yell at me, plain as day, 'I am sorry Mom, I am so sorry, I am sorry Mom!' That's exactly what he would have done. It was his voice, saying it to me." Betty paused.

"That's what Peter said to me, only it was in my dreams," I exclaimed. "He was sorry for what happened and upset because he couldn't return with me into the physical world. My dreams had a definite progression. Peter even gave me advice. He encouraged me to let my grief subside and let me know he was still there to love me as a Soul. It was painful for him to see me suffer."

Betty replied without skipping a beat, "When my children first died, I felt them around all the time. My first son, Wayne, was killed in Vietnam in 1971. Chris was killed in 1983, twelve years later. I asked my guides the day Wayne shipped out for Vietnam, 'Is he going to be all right?' They said, 'Your son will be killed before March 1st.' I thought, 'Oh shit.' He was killed

January 9th. I should never have asked. But I asked, so they told me. Boy, if you don't want to know, don't ask."

I listened intently as Betty told me, "I didn't break down and cry for the first two months. Everyone around me was falling apart, so I couldn't. But after two months I went into the bedroom and had a good cry. When I got up at the end, I saw Wayne standing at the foot of the bed looking at me. He said teasingly, 'Okay Mom, if you're tired of feeling sorry for yourself, why don't you get up and do something constructive.' I was like, 'Okay, I will.' So, I don't allow myself to cry for more than two minutes, that's it. Because I know they are standing and watching."

There was something truly exquisite in this conversation with Betty. Her words—so natural, yet so removed from the norm—reflected my own experiences. Her stories, shared so personally, provided me with the real-life verifications I had so deeply longed for. I felt my solitude, worry, and fears being transformed into an almost matter-of-fact sense of knowing.

A flash of Janet's voice in Israel echoed in my mind, and I asked Betty, "Could you describe your experience of the voice you heard? Was it inside your head or did you hear it outside yourself?"

"It was inside my head, but it was so loud," Betty chuckled. "I could feel Chris near me, up on my right, shouting those words. But no one else in the house heard him because his voice was projected within me. He's always up on the right. Everyone who comes in, they're always up on the right, not on the ground."

"That's what I've come to sense as well," I replied. "When my grandparents appeared, and Peter, they were an energy field above me, yet in the same space with me. The main thing they wanted was to tell me they were okay, that they were in a good place. Did you get that feeling from Chris, as well?"

"He knew that I knew he was okay," said Betty simply. "He knew that because we were talking to each other."

"When Peter appears, I feel a radiance in his Soul presence," I said. "It's like a heavy weight or an energy field in the air. I feel it in my body. It's like the tingling sensation in your hands after you rub them together quickly. It was the same with my grandmother. How do you experience their presence?"

Betty paused as she took another sip of her Pepsi and in a dramatic tone replied, "Oh yes, that's it. It was an energy. I felt Chris. I knew without question that he was there."

We were on a roll, yet the session time was almost up and there was so much more to talk about. I felt a moment's concern that I might leave out something important. Then I decided to let whatever questions popped out of my mouth direct the remainder of the conversation.

"Hey Betty," I said with a child-like inquisitiveness. "When you look back on the days before Chris's death, in hindsight, do you see any signs he might have given you that he knew he had a short life and was preparing you for his death?"

"Oh yeah!" she replied without a trace of doubt. "Chris said to me when he was 19 years old, 'You know Mom, I think I'm going to die young.' And I said, 'Oh that's just your death cycle you feel approaching at 21.' But in retrospect, I would love to have said, 'Chris, how do you know that? How do you feel about that?'"

I was struck by the uncanny parallels in our experiences, and I wanted to share my deepest thoughts before the session ended and hear Betty's response to them.

"You know, Betty," I said, grateful to be having this conversation. "I really believe that the departed know when it's their time to go. I think when we sleep at night, we review our Soul plan, and this knowing lives in our subconscious upon awakening."

"So those who may only be here a brief time," I continued, "know this at a deep level and try to prepare others in advance. They might not consciously know why they say what they do. It just comes through them. They may even get their life in order before leaving, to try and take care of important business beforehand."

"Pete used to tell me he was going to die young," I continued. "I always told him, 'Oh you are going to outlive me.' But the last time he said it, an ominous chill ran through my body. It was the first time I didn't fight him on it. He died soon thereafter. Now I know that he really knew."

"Yeah, the day that Chris died, I said to him, 'What do you want for your birthday?' His birthday was May 24, and this was on April 8. I said, 'Do you want a new windshield for your motorcycle?' He looked up at me and said, 'Oh Mom, that's a long time from now, I may not even be alive.' He was killed two hours later. To top it off, he had his income taxes done so I could go in and finish it up. He did such an excellent job, what an organized kid. He was so young and had it all done."

Betty and I gazed deeply into each other's eyes with an upwelling of emotion, and said at the same time, "Amazing!"

Then we had a good laugh.

One last thought came to mind as the session ended. Betty continued with me, graciously allowing our session to go over-time.

"Betty, on a couple of occasions I've experienced departed loved ones appearing at their own burial service. It was so helpful and reassuring, but it was also hard because I was the only one who knew it. I wished everyone could have had the experience. The signs are so subtle. We're not taught to perceive them, but they are there."

"Yeah, you can feel them there, can't you?" she said. "If you look at a body in a casket it's always an empty shell. Nobody is there. I think it's good that we look, so we can see it's empty and nobody is there. Then maybe we can try to feel our loved one with us as a spiritual presence."

I said, "Yeah, and it's tough for the departed, too! They're with us saying, 'Hey, I'm here. I'm with you now.' But if we don't know how to feel them or become sensitive to the signs, then we don't know they are there."

"Children feel and see their departed loved ones more easily," said Betty. "As they grow older, it gets harder. But younger kids naturally have their sixth sense open, and they will say, 'Grandpa came and talked to me.'"

"So, as we get older, we start losing our sixth sense?" I asked.

"Yes, unless we start meditating to awaken it again. The more creative and sensitive people are, the more they rely on the power of the sixth sense whether they realize it or not. But a large percent of the population is spiritually blind because their spiritual eye is no longer open. That is going to change—many more people will be going on a spiritual journey, an inner journey, much like you and me. But it often takes unusual or difficult experiences to catalyze our awakening."

"When we lose a loved one, it starts to wake us up," Betty continued. "We begin to question the nature and purpose of life and death. It changed my life and my way of seeing life. We may never think deeply about these things until something painful happens to us. So that is our wake-up call. It makes us stop and ask, 'If there is no death, what am I doing here? What is life about?'"

Betty's concluding thoughts beautifully set a closing tone.

"Wow! That's so true!" I said. "My life hasn't been the same since the passing of my family members. After each death I started living and seeing in a new way. Now my mission is to learn more about and fulfill my higher purpose for being here."

It was time to go. As I grabbed the cassette tape of our conversation, Betty lovingly repeated what she says at the end of every session, "Don't forget to meditate so your energy stays up!"

I closed the door behind me, grateful at having found the spiritual companionship and confirmation I had been longing for.

That would be the last time I'd see Betty. She passed away July 30, 2002.

The insights pouring out from Betty Bethards and the Inner Light Foundation were part of a larger movement ushering in a new age of enlightenment. It was a perfect time to ride the wave.

However, Betty's parting admonition—"Don't forget to meditate!"—suddenly had a powerful impact on me.

Meditation had always given me much-needed healing and inner peace, but after returning from Israel, my meditation practice wavered under the pressures and demands of daily life. When Peter's death plunged me into an abyss of grief and sorrow, I began to meditate regularly, but eventually work demands had pulled me away again.

While driving home on the freeway that afternoon, Betty's counseling inspired me to reflect on the effect meditation had had on my life. There was one amazing experience in particular that I pulled up from the memory banks—while still making sure I carefully navigated through the traffic.

It was a morning meditation session I had noted in my journal during which Pete had appeared to my inner vision several months after passing.

I remembered how in my vision, Pete grabbed my hand and led me, in my Soul body, through a forest to a log cabin—his apparent residence in the afterlife. When we entered the cabin, he began to leap and spin in joyous circles. He looked like a young, happy version of his 27-year-old self.

I remembered how I didn't respond to Pete, just watched with joy; How his spirit was free, with no trace of the anxiety and despair that had often made his life on earth difficult; How his joy was contagious, as he exclaimed, "Lu, Lu, I am so happy! I am learning so much! You can't believe how much I'm learning! You know all that stuff you told me and showed me and read to me? Well...I know it now! It's *everything* to me now! It was all I needed. I *love* myself now. I can see the good I did on earth."

I remembered how ecstatic he was and how we had looked into each other's eyes, smiling joyfully, and how the vision ended just as I had come to the end of my meditation session.

Still reflecting, my gas gauge was near empty, so I pulled over at the nearest gas station. Then I remembered how Pete had stayed with Dan and Terri at their Rivendell log cabin when he was 13 years old. The fact he had taken me to a log cabin during my meditation session made so much sense.

Stunned by the profundity of this meditation experience, I continued to reflect while waiting for the tank to fill. I remembered how a few minutes after my meditation session ended, Tamarin woke up and walked sleepily into my room.

"What are you doing?" she asked.

"I just finished meditating," I remembered saying.

"I want to do that," Tam said.

Only 7-years-old at the time, Tamarin was an eager little Soul.

I remembered how she quietly sat beside me, closed her eyes, and let go of the world for a few minutes. Then she opened her eyes and looked up at me.

"Mommy, I saw Papa!" she said excitedly. "He was in a cabin in the woods with red decorations all around the room. He was happy to see me! We hugged, and then I was here again."

Reflecting on this experience gave me goose bumps. Tamarin had seen Peter's spirit in the cabin!

I remembered how I had told her about my vision and how we hugged for what seemed like hours.

It was inspiring to remember how meditation had always proven to be the medicine I needed to heal the grief and sense of loss that had plagued my life. Meditation had brought me peace, and further opened my sixth sense. Over time, my meditation experiences had even filled several journals.

So, now I knew it was time to reestablish a regular practice.

This time, however, I combined the Laya Yoga I had practiced in Israel with Betty's twenty-minute meditation regimen.

Laya Yoga awakens higher states of consciousness through contemplation of specific energy centers in the body. Betty's method, an ancient Egyptian technique passed down to her by her teachers, incorporates affirmations, visualizations, and white light.

This combination is extremely powerful. I was now daily exercising the muscle of my attention—the doorway to the sixth sense—that had weakened from lack of use. As I did so, the eyes of my Soul opened wider.

My prayers for deeper metaphysical understanding, and for the supportive companionship of spiritual peers, continued to be answered, often in surprising ways. As I continued to build my career, my vow to not only meditate regularly but to also share with others the insights I had learned about the power of the Soul within grew more urgent.

Through my dreams and meditations, a new light of understanding was shed on the simple purpose of my sojourn here on earth. I saw how all of the events in my life fit in, even the challenging situations, the tragic events, and the negative emotions and limitations of my personality.

Answers to "Who am I?" and "What is My Higher Purpose?" solidified even further.

We are not only multi-dimensional beings with six senses—a personality and a Soul—but also everything we have to endure is part of the plan for our life. It's all useful; all "grist for the mill."

Our task is to name the specific emotions we came here to master—to reverse engineer our Soul plan—and then use all of our experiences and limitations to integrate our personality with our Soul.

The goal is to evolve as a Soul—as the Beings of Light had said—and although this sounded great in theory, I had no idea the amount of discipline it would actually require.

I did know however, that it was one thing to experience the peace of meditation in the comfort of my home, but it was another to maintain that same Soul consciousness while in the world facing my emotions.

So, I continued to expand my Soul Fitness Program into a specific 7-Step exercise program to access and live my Soul's wisdom. I trademarked this program Soulercise®, and self-published my material in 2004 as *Soulercise — 7 Steps to Exercise Your Soul and Master Daily Life*. I became a part-time Soul coach, teaching clients to Soulercise and manifesting the messages from the Beings of Light—22 years later! The 2nd edition, *Soul Bridges*, is now part of *The Soul Series* books.

CHAPTER 20

Will and Determination

With the 7 Steps now in my pocket, I was determined to unveil the full contents of my Soul plan. It was time to walk the walk and Soulercise while grappling with yet another major challenge—Tamarin's medical crises.

They started when Tam was 4 years old.

While running around the swings on her preschool playground one afternoon, a boy was swinging fast and high. At just the wrong moment, Tam passed in front of him. Unable to stop, his foot struck her hard on the side of the head, knocking her unconscious.

I rushed Tam to the doctor's office where, after a brief examination, I was assured that she was fine. Since she wasn't throwing up or displaying other symptoms of concussion, she was sent home.

There, Tamarin remained unconscious for seven long hours. When she woke up it seemed that, indeed, she was fine.

Tam resumed an active childhood. Her ballet and gymnastics classes confirmed that she was gifted at both. At 10 years old, she combined these two disciplines, and became a rhythmic gymnast. Watching her agile routines with either a hoop, ball, ribbon, or clubs was breathtaking.

Tamarin's long hours at the gym paid off, because two years later she was the Rhythmic Gymnastics National Champion in the Children's division. Her dream of making the USA Rhythmic Gymnastics National team and competing in the Olympics seemed within reach— until life placed an obstacle in the middle of her path.

It was shortly before Tamarin's 14th birthday that she was diagnosed with type 1 diabetes.

Tam took the news like a true champion and refused to give up her dream. For the next few years, she managed her diabetes and continued her rigorous training schedule.

During the 1991 National Championships, Tam made the USA Junior National Team. She now competed both nationally and internationally. In 1992 she was the USA Bronze medalist at the Louvain La Neuve 4 Continents Championships in Brussels, Belgium!

Eventually, however, Tam's diabetes took an increasing toll on her body, and she decided to no longer continue training as an elite gymnast.

In true Tamarin style, she soon devised another plan. Tam auditioned for and joined the Nike-sponsored Hip Hop dance troupe, Culture Shock San Francisco.

At 18 years old Tamarin, moved to New York and became co-director/choreographer for Culture Shock New York while studying fashion design at FIT. Her choreography was presented at Madison Square Garden and the U.S. Open, while her fashions were featured in FIT's end-of-the-year fashion show—major achievements for a 19-year-old.

In her early 20s, Tamarin's diabetes began careening out of control. After going into diabetic ketoacidosis (DKA—a diabetic coma) several times, she attended diabetes management classes. Still, no matter how hard Tam tried, her blood sugars were continually outside the normal range.

Tamarin also started having problems focusing on subjects and following conversations. So, we had her return to California, where she could be close to home while getting evaluated at several local clinics. Eventually Tam was diagnosed as bipolar and put on medications that made things worse. Around this same time, alcohol rehab centers across the country had expanded their services to include mental health/dual diagnosis treatment. It was a perfect solution.

We enrolled her in a local facility where a team of doctors could decide on the right cocktail of medications for her bipolar disorder.

After several weeks, Michael and I were called in for a meeting with the executive team.

"Tamarin is not bipolar," the director said matter-of-factly.

It was the last thing we expected to hear.

"We've worked with hundreds of bipolar patients, and Tamarin does not fit the model," she explained. "She has trouble processing information. Has she ever had a head injury?"

"Yes!" I immediately recalled the swing incident. "She was knocked unconscious for seven hours when she was 4 years old!"

The director nodded in confirmation. "You need to take her to see a neurologist right away."

A SPECT scan revealed that Tam had a mild traumatic brain injury (mTBI). Her playground injury as a 4-year-old, and subsequent car and snowboarding accidents, had caused axonal shearing or tearing of the brain's long connecting nerve fibers (axons).

These factors accounted for her cognitive deficits—confusion, problems with judgment, difficulties managing diabetes, disinhibition, and emotional imbalance. Finally, it all made sense.

For years, Tam's disturbing and inexplicable symptoms had put me through cycles of worry and fear. Once again, a battle raged between my personality and my Soul. I was relieved now that we finally had the right diagnosis, but it also triggered a new wave of painful thoughts and emotions of worry and fear.

They flooded through me most prominently when I saw Tamarin desperately struggling with her symptoms. Remorseful thoughts plagued me, "If only I had picked Tam up from preschool earlier.... If I hadn't gone to L.A. this never would have happened."

Now, however, I was a bit more skilled at holding enlightened perspectives.

"Wait! It's time to see this from a more positive light," I encouraged myself.

Then I chose a higher Soul thought to anchor in my consciousness and replace my fear.

I reminded myself, "This is how her life was meant to go—there's a higher purpose; this was our Soul Agreement!"

After that, every time I was fearful, I remembered my Soul thought and visualized its enlightened perspective and the higher reality from which it emanated.

It worked!

Every time I practiced; I felt a new sense of trust. Under the supervision of my Soul, my fear diminished.

Discovering the cause of Tamarin's symptoms brought a sense of relief. It wasn't a cure, but at least we knew what we were dealing with. Tamarin was prescribed new medications that seemed to help. However, sadly, over time they lost their effectiveness and periodic increases in dosage were needed.

Now 29 years old, Tamarin didn't give up. She tried to build a career as a fashion consultant and a make-up artist. Even with the medications, she found it difficult to hold jobs and make effective decisions.

So, I began to research ways to heal mTBI—called the "invisible disability"—without medication. I travelled around the country interviewing the top Neuroscientists and leaders in the field of EEG Biofeedback (Neurofeedback).

I found a Neurofeedback program that seemed promising and paid for Tam's training to heal her head injury.

I was so impressed with the results that I committed myself to learning and using these remarkable innovative technologies. Eventually, I sold my stocks, left the computer industry, and created my own NeuroFitness training center—NeuroFit Marin.

My goal was to make this invisible disability visible and manageable—and not just in Tamarin's case. It had taken us seven years to get Tam accurately diagnosed. If I could help other families shave even a year off that time, then I knew that everything we went through was worth it.

At NeuroFit, Tamarin continued to enhance the neuroplasticity of her brain. The neuro-magic worked, and her condition was improving.

Then her diabetes hit a point of no return. In 2012, Tam went into end-stage renal failure. Her kidney was almost gone, and she now required dialysis four hours a day, four days a week. Eventually Tamarin needed a new kidney, so I decided to undergo testing.

Results showed that I was a tissue and blood type match, so I agreed to donate my kidney to Tam. However, that plan changed dramatically when our endless roller coaster ride took yet another abrupt turn.

As the date of our operations approached, the hospital called to let Tam know that a kidney had become available. It had belonged to an anonymous 18-year-old girl who had just died in a car accident. Tamarin rushed to UCSF for the surgery, and she received not only the girl's kidney, but her pancreas as well—a double transplant! It was a miracle.

Now 36 years old, Tamarin no longer had kidney disease or diabetes. She no longer needed dialysis or the insulin injections she had required since she was 13 years old. After going through a year of organ rejection and subsequent hospitalizations, Tam's new organs and medication regiment finally took hold.

Everything seemed to be working out. Tamarin was better and NeuroFit was going strong. I had developed a "Cross-Train Your Brain" program that incorporated Soulercise into the brain, body, and mind fitness programs. I was teaching people to Soulercise, including myself—the opportunity to practice what I preached was never too far away!

The symptoms of Tamarin's mTBI were now well understood. However, over the next four years, medical issues continued to both challenge Tam and challenge me to live with higher perspectives.

My Soul Fitness Program—to shift from personality consciousness to Soul consciousness—required disciplined inner work. It required a dedication like that of an elite athlete, an accomplished musician, or a master craftsman. All I could do was practice and try my best.

I also knew that visualization and positive affirmations alone could not accomplish this. Higher guidance was also needed and always available, but it was up to me to develop the inner discipline of tuning into this guidance through prayer, meditation, reflection, and through my dreams. But that, too, was not always easy.

The will and determination to forge a relationship between my Soul and personality, became my focus. I knew Soul fitness would help me find my equilibrium in times of crisis whenever disturbing thoughts and emotions threatened to overwhelm me. It would help me transform the negative patterns of my human personality and live the enlightened perspectives of my Soul. Most importantly, there were always plenty of opportunities to practice.

In parallel to Tam's medical challenges, my mom was now nearing her end of life. She had moved to Saratoga Springs, New York to live in assisted living near Debby and Carol. It had been a wonderful next stage of life for her. Debby found a perfect apartment that Mom decorated in classic Vevie style with works of art and beautiful furniture she had brought from her Los Angeles condo. Mom met new friends and lived a life full of bridge games, cocktail parties, fun visits with Debby, and wonderful meals.

As old age ran its course, Mom's health quickly took a turn for the worse. Now 87 years old, it was time to move to an acute care facility. This was no life for Vevie, and it didn't take long for her health to turn critical. I flew out to New York and was grateful to spend a day with Mom while she was still alive.

When my dad had passed away, I remembered his last words were, "Good night, or goodbye, or whatever you call it!" By the time I arrived to see my mom, she was no longer awake or speaking.

I was grateful for the hospice nurse who told us, "talk to your mom because the last thing to go is our hearing. She may not be able to see you or respond to you, but she can hear you and knows you are there."

Debby and I spent the rest of the day with mom, sitting by her side talking close to her ear. A couple of times we noticed a twitch or two when we'd say something to her. It was a gesture that we were sure meant she had indeed heard us.

As late night approached, Debby and I had said all there was to say. We didn't want to go but knew it was time. We gave Mom one last hug and reluctantly left.

Debby and I drove the twenty-minutes back to her house and poured a glass of wine to share and reflect with Carol. It wasn't long after our arrival that the call came in.

Mom had passed.

We woke up early the next morning and drove to the care center. Mom was still in her same room while arrangements were being made for her cremation. The wonderful hospice nurse was also still there, and I will never forget what she told us.

She lovingly said, "It is common for loved ones to wait until you are gone to take their last breath and pass away. It's as if they don't want to die in front of you." She then walked over to the other side of the room and said, "I am opening this window so your mom's Soul can fly free."

I felt so grateful for the nurses' care and for being there with Debby to see Mom one last time. I stayed in New York for a few more days as we finalized arrangements and visited with family and friends. It was a wonderful farewell.

My long flight home provided plenty of time for reflection. I remembered the good times with Mom, her wonderful laugh, and her uncanny ability to entertain friends with fabulous gourmet meals.

I thought about how each death in the family had brought with it an awakening and a new sense of enlightenment. Then right on cue, my thoughts turned to Betty Bethards and our last conversation.

I specifically remembered when I asked Betty, "If you were to give a message to anyone out in the world, what would it be?"

Betty responded without hesitation, "That there is no death!"

I reflected once more on Betty's belief that when we lose a loved one it makes us wake up and to so many questions like: "What is life? What is death? What am I doing here? And What is life about?"

I knew I would never stop asking those questions!

As I continued to reflect on my last meeting with Betty, I remembered how I had shared with her a conversation between Tam and I after Pete's passing. Tam was still processing his death at the time and had shared the most beautiful sentiment with me.

Tam told me, "If you haven't experienced death, you haven't gotten the full benefit of what it is to have someone on the other side."

I loved Betty's reply, "Yes, that is true. To me the most important thing is knowing they are standing there watching us and can hear our thoughts, words, and actions. If we are sitting there crying and wallowing in it, they have to sit there and watch, and it hurts them. The same thing when we go out to the graveyard. They are not there in the ground. You can be at home and visit them. That is where they are!"

As the plane continued west towards San Francisco, I sat back in my chair, closed my eyes and felt the benefit of having my loved ones on the other side. I said, "hi" to Pete, gave Mom a virtual hug, and I silently called out to Dad, "good night!"

Back in Marin, I returned to work and felt thankful that my clients at NeuroFit were understanding of my time away and simply grateful to continue their training.

Then, once again, I was shaken to the core.

During her time on dialysis, Tamarin had developed blood clots that eventually caused a stroke. A few months later she was diagnosed with a 7 lb. malignant ovarian tumor. Even though I knew these challenging moments and the fear they generated were an opportunity to practice the enlightened reality in which I wanted to live, it was not easy to maintain trust in the face of this fear.

While waiting for word on Tam's surgery to remove the tumor, I practiced replacing agitation and fear with calming thoughts that generated trust. I was reprogramming myself to shift from a negative personality viewpoint to an elevated Soul perspective—the place I so wanted to be.

It was a nail-biter, but finally word came—the surgery was successful. The USCF surgeon called it a best-case scenario! Tam was released into an acute care facility to recuperate.

During these latest medical emergencies, I noticed it was getting a bit easier to recognize the negative thought patterns when they arose, to put on the brakes and stop them in their tracks. It felt rewarding to embrace the emotion they generated and then consciously shift to the Soul thoughts I wanted to make my reality.

Soon it became apparent that although each situation brought with it a new set of challenges, there were no new emotions. The same emotions appeared over and over in different situations, giving me a change to practice transforming them.

I had finally identified the emotions I came here to master. I had discovered the full contents of my Soul Plan!

There was no rest for the weary, however, when once again medical issues stepped in. The doctors determined that a blood clot had now travelled to Tamarin's transplanted kidney and killed it. Her kidney had also become infected and was surgically removed. A few months later, her pancreas also failed, and she went into a coma. Multiple insulin injections brought her back into a conscious state.

When Tam woke up, she looked around the room, and said, "I didn't die." "I don't want to die." "Don't let me die!" Her will and determination to live was amazing.

During these traumatic times, I continued to practice what I preached. I constantly reached into the depths of my Soul and applied my own will and determination to not give in to my fears.

As hard as it was at times, I really did find strength from my Soul. It was one thing to know that we are both a personality and a Soul, but another to follow my Soul's voice over the lure of my personality in times of trouble. I must admit, it was a tug-of-war, but I did my best to continue and walk the walk.

I watched in amazement while dialysis and insulin kept Tam alive. Although she was critically ill, Tamarin continued with the same will and determination that had made her a competitive gymnast. Tam faced each crisis and ongoing medical emergency square on.

As for me, the more I Soulercised, the easier it became to override patterns that had previously controlled and limited me. Bit by bit, my Soul was becoming my life partner, and my growth began to accelerate.

The path that our Souls agreed to and signed up in for this lifetime allowed Tam and I to be each other's teacher. Tam's medical challenges blessed us with the ultimate lesson we all experience as human beings, which is surrender. Surrender to the higher lessons and trust—trust that everything is unfolding for the highest good; trust in something invisible; trust that our Soul chooses things for us that can look terrible on the outside but end up being our perfect Soul plan for what we came here to learn.

Tam's medical conditions broke us wide open and took us to that place of surrender. For that I am so grateful.

CHAPTER 21

Personal Victory

Tragedy had swirled around me since I was 12 years old, but now it was almost a daily occurrence. Tamarin's medical crises continued to escalate, so it was time to seek help—in true Cindy style.

During the ongoing challenges in my life, I had begun to solicit the aid of psychics—individuals who use the power of extrasensory perception, or sixth sense, to identify information beyond our normal five senses.

Amongst an abundance of helpful discussions, one psychic told me that I'd be living in a log cabin. I thought the only way that would happen was if I moved to the Montana wilderness. So, it didn't make any sense at the time. Fast forward 29 years. I began dating Rob and eventually moved into a house he'd built on his grandfather's property. It was a log cabin in the middle of Marin County, CA!

Another psychic I had met at the Renaissance Faire when I was 31 years old, gave me a "Life Cycle" reading. He told me, "In the 4th Segment of your life you will open a Center that will be a great source of healing for many people."

At the time, it seemed completely far-fetched. But here I am, 27 years after his vision, founder of NeuroFit Marin—a healing center for the brain!

These readings are astounding to think about. Like Janet, these psychics had access to my Soul plan years before the events actually manifested in my life.

Now, with Tamarin's health emergencies skyrocketing out of control, once again I needed help to find a higher perspective. Why were we on such a difficult path? What was the higher purpose at work here? What was our Soul Agreement?

For answers, I sought the aid of a Vedic astrologer—a Hindu form of astrology, mediums—individuals who communicate between Souls of the living and the dead, and a trance channeler—an individual who goes into a meditative state or trance and allows spirit beings to speak through him.

Each provided the answers I was seeking.

Medium channel Leanne Rosko Doty teaches that we are more than the sum of our parts, we are consciousness shining through a physical body. When I contacted Leanne for a higher perspective on all Tam and I were going through, she said:

> *"The main goal in Tamarin's Soul Chart this lifetime is Soul growth. And the easiest way for us to grow is through all the things that she is facing-just one after another. When you were sitting with your teachers and planning this life out, she was like, 'Okay, I am going to take the bull by the horns in this next life, are you up for the medical challenges I'll face?' And the warrior spirit in you said, 'Heck yes!' That became the essence of your contract with each other."*

When I was pregnant with Tamarin, I did pray for a Soul to come into this life through me who would help others. With no memory of our pre-incarnation agreement, I did not ask for a Soul without critical life-threatening illnesses. Later I would joke that we need to be specific in what we ask for!

Leanne's reading did provide a higher perspective for us to hold on to—Soul growth.

In the midst of Tamarin's mounting medical issues, and her survival of multiple near-death events, I was continually being told how inspirational she was, and that her life story needed to be told.

I often asked myself, "Doesn't there have to be a happy ending? And why are so many people encouraging me to share Tam's story?"

For answers, I consulted Kevin Ryerson. A renowned trance channeler in the tradition of Edgar Cayce, Kevin is also an expert intuitive. He has been a guest on many television shows, including *Oprah* and *Good Morning America*, and is the author of the landmark book, *Spirit Communications: The Soul's Path*.

When I read Shirley MacLaine's bestseller *Out on a Limb*, I noted how she praised Kevin's psychic skills. I knew that Kevin Ryerson would be an excellent resource, and here's what he had to say:

> *"Given your prayer for a Soul to be born to help others .... Are you aware of the case history of Helen Keller who lost her sight and hearing following a serious illness as an infant? Our prayers sometimes have an unexpected way of transpiring, and your prayer is very much in the Helen Keller category. In fact, there are many parallels between your daughter's story and Helen Keller.*

Helen changed many attitudes and lives, even though she didn't experience a complete healing herself. It could be that because you wanted a soul to incarnate who would help others, maybe you have the Helen Keller-like Soul here—that people could learn from her story.

I have witnessed many complete healings, based on prayers, but that is not always the case. Classic happy endings may or may not happen. Even if your daughter is not a complete beneficiary of a healing, she may already be serving her Soul's purpose. Helen Keller Soul types can have a powerful impact on so many other lives. Nine times out of ten, when they do pass on, they come to the realization that their life had a higher purpose. This might be the case with your daughter."

As Tamarin faced new challenges, the notion of a happy ending to her story now took on new meaning. It was no longer so much about a complete personal healing for her—although I continued to pray for help—as it was about being of service and fulfilling her purpose along the way.

Tam stretched medical teams to the limits of their knowledge. What they learned from her numerous, complex health issues improved the care they could now offer other patients.

Her relentless challenges had pushed my coping capacity to new extremes, yet I was also given opportunity after opportunity to overcome my fear and to live in the Soul-state of trust. Additionally, Tamarin's life-changing head injury all those years ago has helped countless other families through NeuroFit Marin.

Whatever might happen next, surely, Tamarin had already fulfilled her Soul's purpose.

It was during a NeuroFit training session that one of my

clients told me about a Vedic Astrologer named Joni Patry. I contacted Joni, hoping for another resource to help me see a higher perspective on Tam's life.

During the hour-long reading, I realized how closely Vedic Astrology reflects the content of our Soul plan. It's astounding. Joni proceeded to pinpoint the exact time frame for each major medical crisis in Tam's life—some of which hadn't even occurred yet!

Joni mentioned the extreme stress Tamarin's ailments placed on her organs and said that now her heart was weakening. I told her how I often saw Tamarin as a Soul, and was resigned to the reality that, at some point, she would be done with her body and be free and happy. Meanwhile, she was still trucking along day after day, never complaining, not even when she had to do dialysis again.

Joni described Tam's iron will to live and detailed the many times she'd been at death's door. A family joke was that Tamarin didn't have nine lives; she had 42 lives!

The most stunning moments came when I asked Joni, "This is crazy. How much can one human Soul endure in a lifetime?" Joni replied:

> "This was your destiny to do this together. To be honest, I am a little surprised that Tamarin is still here. She is hanging on for dear life. She doesn't want to leave. You know, I seldom predict the end of physical life. Instead, I usually talk about a specific point in time and how difficult it may or may not be.
>
> Whether Tam is still here or not, let me give you a date that is significant for her. I am looking at November 14th. November is the month when she may ultimately be free.

However, she may linger on the astral plane for quite some time while trying to help you. You will definitely have visions of her and connections with her. She will be doing things that are definitely manifestations in this world to give you proof that she is still nearby and her love for you runs deep and true.

Wow, that is going to be so wonderful. Tam is going to have her strength back. She is going to feel good again. She is going to be in direct communication. As a matter of fact, I think talking with her will be easier than ever before. That will be part of your experience in writing. Then once she leaves the astral plane, she'll move on to higher realms."

For the next year, the date November 14th sat in the back of my mind. Tam and I simply soldiered on through each crises, until October 23, 2020. While at work that afternoon, I received a call from the dialysis center. They were concerned about Tamarin's heart. Her blood pressure had dropped precipitously, and an ambulance had taken her to the ER.

Searching for answers to this latest medical development, her doctor ordered a CT scan. The pictures arrived the next morning, revealing a huge mass in her pelvic area—a 9-inch 15 lb. tumor was attached to her colon.

Due to COVID, it took almost two weeks for a bed to become available at UCSF, but finally Tamarin was transferred to the Mission Bay Hospital. Given the situation, she was in relatively good spirits and looking forward to having the tumor surgically removed.

On Tuesday, November 10th, in a Zoom meeting with her surgeon, Tam received devastating news. The tumor had grown arteries and veins and was inoperable. If it were removed, she would bleed to death. Without warning, once again the goal changed. They would adjust Tamarin's pain medication and release her in a few days.

Her response after the meeting was classic Tam: "Well *that* wasn't very good news!"

Three days later, Tamarin's tumor became infected, and she was placed in ICU on IV antibiotics. On November 14th—the Vedic Astrology date when "something happens for her"—we had to make the tough decision to set her free.

The head nurse came in and told us Tamarin's heart had weakened to the point where dialysis was no longer possible. At a doctor's meeting later that morning, they encouraged Michael and me to take her off all IVs and keep her comfortable. We reluctantly agreed—it was the best option for her.

Tam never regained consciousness.

One miraculous event did happen the next afternoon. After not speaking for almost a full day, Tam suddenly opened her eyes and said, "There's a temple in the sky, and everything is reverberating!"

Wow! We knew then that she was going to a good place.

Four hours later, on November 15, 2020, at 8:38 p.m., Tamarin gracefully took her last breath and crossed over into the light. With her astounding last words echoing through my mind, peace washed over me. I could see her in the Sky Temple with Pete and the Beings of Light.

Tam had finally left her weary body behind. Her Soul was alive and free. She was home again!

For years Tamarin had fought for her life, demonstrating a strength and resiliency that inspired all who knew her. Several of her friends told me the same thing, "When I think my life is tough, all I have to do is think about Tam and I realize I don't have it so bad."

When I picked up Tamarin's ashes the following week from Monte's Chapel of the Hills, I had to sign her death certificate. The cause of death was written as Ovarian Cancer, but to my surprise it also contained a laundry list of the additional medical afflictions from which she had suffered. Even so, it wasn't a complete list.

The coroner, who was a family friend, handed me her documents with a look of disbelief. "If anyone comes in here complaining about their life," he said, "I should show them this death certificate!"

With the to-do list around Tam's passing now complete, I transitioned back into everyday life. As I did, I often wondered what Tamarin is up to now, and watched excitedly to see in what form her after-death presence would appear.

Having experienced Janet's presence in Israel, Honey's presence in San Diego, and Pete's after his passing, my Soul was turning towards Tamarin, like a compass seeking true north. I knew she would find a way to make her presence known.

I had asked my dad years earlier what animal he wanted to come back as to make his after-death presence known. Since he and Jeanne lived on the coast at the time, his answer was instant—a pelican. However, they had moved inland, and after I watched my dad take his last breath, I sat on their back patio to grieve. With tears running down my cheek, an owl began to hoot from the tree above me.

"Dad," I whispered to myself. "Are you here through the owl?" The owl hooted back, yet I still wasn't sure until each morning for the next two days, Jeanne found an owl feather at the front door!

It didn't take long for Tam to make her presence known.

A few days after she passed, I was outside on the phone with Shanan Martin, Tam's childhood gymnastics buddy. As we talked, a hawk landed high in the redwood tree above me. At the same moment, an egret landed on the roof above Shanan. It was a simultaneous Tamarin sighting.

Later I looked up the spiritual symbolism of both birds, and here's what I found: Egrets teach us to stand in the spiritual and physical worlds, while hawks act as divine messengers that carry Souls between the physical and spiritual realms.

Wow! Excellent choice, Tam!

The next day I parked by the San Francisco Bay. While eating lunch, I called on Tam Soul to Soul, trying to initiate contact with her, the same way I had done with Pete.

A group of ducks swam in front of me. I laughed, "What Tam, are you going to appear as a duck and waddle over to say hi?"

Just then, a hawk flew in and perched on top of a nearby wooden post. It stared at me. I took a picture, marveling at the synchronicity, as goose bumps formed on my arms and chills ran up my spine. I was no longer surprised. Instead, I allowed myself to merge with her presence.

We embraced in an energy hug. The exchange was so precious that time seemed to stand still. A woman and her dog walked by, and the hawk flew onto the roof of a nearby building. It maintained eye contact with me until I finished eating.

I had brought a box of Tam's photo albums to keep in our storage unit next door. As I returned to the car, carrying the empty box, I noticed a memento still stuck inside. The words written on it went straight to my heart. They simply said, "You are Loved."

As I drove home a beautiful heart-shaped cloud formed over Mt. Tam. I pulled over to take a picture as profound emotions welled up in me.

"I love you too, Tam!"

Hooting owls outside my window....perfectly timed brilliant rainbows stretching from horizon to horizon in front of me.... cloud formations that spelled "Hi"....even meaningful license plates and other significant occurrences....were ways Tam continued to reach out to remain a vibrant presence in my life.

Plans for Tam's celebration of life were delayed by COVID, but on her birthday, a few close friends and I took a physically distanced walk along the Bay. I showed them the post where the hawk had kept me company, and we were all looking to the sky, hoping for another sign of Tamarin.

It didn't take long. At the end of our walk, a lone jet appeared in blue sky above us. As it disappeared behind the hills, its jet vapor formed a massive cloud-like rainbow that reached from horizon to horizon!

"Hi Tam!" we shouted in unison.

One of Tamarin's last requests was to return to Hawaii and swim with the dolphins again. I kept my promise and sent a portion of ashes to her godfather, Dana. From his boat off Waikiki, Tam was released into the ocean to swim with the dolphins. Of course, the ceremony was blessed with another massive rainbow. Sent by Tam, it stretched over both Waikiki and Diamond Head—her spiritual home.

These Tamarin sightings were a blessing, and a balm for my grief. That she could cross over and immediately use her energy to affect the physical realm is a testament to her strength.

Mediums have confirmed that she is comfortable in the

afterlife and has released her attachment to the earth plane, yet she continues to visit.

Long conversations with family, and multiple reconnections with Tamarin's friends, were also tremendous sources of healing. The celebratory Facebook Group created in her honor is also a testament to the many lives Tam's Soul touched.

Tamarin took on a lot in her life, but her obstacles and the challenges we faced were the opportunities for growth we had set up before incarnating. The fact that the November 14th date of her disconnection from the physical realm was written in the stars, in her Vedic Astrology Chart, gives further credence to the notion that we come into this life with a Soul plan, and with a particular mission to fulfill.

Tamarin chose her difficult path as the fastest route to expand her light, evolve as a Soul, and help others along the way. Many Souls choose lives with great adversity to contribute to the greater good—to the evolution of a particular field on earth, or to offer maximum growth potential and Soul transcendence. Tam's mission encompassed both. She gave everything she had to the bitter end and completed her mission.

Knowing all of this did provide a big picture perspective in which all the painful, seemingly disparate pieces of Tamarin's life, and mine, formed a purposeful pattern of divine meaning and beauty.

But it did not end the grieving process.

At the nine-month mark of her passing, we had a beautiful celebration of life ceremony and party. Afterwards a deep sadness overcame me. Grief had finally caught up with me and feelings emerged I had never experienced. Often, I didn't even want to leave the house or talk to anyone.

I was advised to, "Just let yourself go through the grieving process." I understood but felt there was a fine line between going through it and staying in it.

My grief became a powerful force that threatened to sink me into overwhelming depression and despair. I'd be fine, and then suddenly sadness would well up from the depths within and possess me. I found myself crying at the thought of hugging Tam's physical body; the memory of her laughter ringing in my ears; or at the sight of her little black leather backpack hanging on my office wall. I read about the stages of grief and while talking to Debby realized I must be in the grief to get through it.

I knew I had done everything humanly possible to help Tam and be there for her. This time, thoughts of what I could have done differently were not present, as they were for Pete. It was the seeming loss of Tam that deeply saddened me. It was the thoughts of not having her to spend holidays with or not being there to love and care for me as I aged that filled me with grief.

It was time to continue and move on. I Soulercised and embraced my thoughts, for they are a relevant part of me. I coached myself to go higher and deeper within and find a new perspective to hold on to as I confirmed the contents of my own Soul Plan.

I heard the voice of my Soul say: "She is free." "She feels good again." "She accomplished her mission." When I replaced thoughts of my loss with these higher Soul perspectives—a feeling of joy replaced the sadness. It was a personal victory!

Next the universe stepped in to help even further. A childhood friend called me and during our conversation, she said, "You've got to contact the medium George Lugo. He's amazing."

So, I did. The first thing George asked was, "Who is on the other side that you took care of? She is saying, 'Thank you.'"

I knew that he was talking to Tamarin, and I listened intently. At one point he said:

> *"She is with you all the time. She hasn't really left you, in the sense that just physically but not really. She says she can do things physically around you and brings you little gifts to let you know she's okay. She did push the envelope. With all her suffering she was a teacher, she taught a lot of things to a lot of people.*
>
> *She says you've cried a river over her, and she is trying to help you back. She says celebrate my life. You don't let it rule you, so that is good. But be sure to celebrate my life, rather than mourn my life. Don't forget to celebrate."*

I am thankful for this message. Yes, I have cried endless tears over Tamarin. Her passing remains bittersweet, and I miss her terribly. Equally true, I don't let it rule me. I know the sadness I feel is natural, yet I am able to celebrate Tam's extraordinary life, while I honor her beautiful Soul. I can Soulercise the sadness when it comes, and all the Soul growth we accomplished remains a source of comfort.

I continue to feel her presence, and I am able to acknowledge the beauty, courage, wisdom, and light of the Being she is. I feel immense gratitude to have shared a mission with such a remarkable Soul, and to have learned that we do not die; death is not the end of our journey. Instead, it is a transition into a new relationship, rich in dimensions beyond this physical world. My relationship with Tamarin continues to grow, and she remains an essential part of each day.

Tam will always inspire me, and I am filled with the desire

for her life to inspire others. Friends and family continue to encourage me to write about her life and her indomitable spirit, still saying that her story needs to be told. The thought does bring comfort, as well as an opportunity for us to be together again. So, yes, her story will be told, and her biography is planned as part of *The Soul Series* books.

My struggles and challenges, and all the emotions of fear and insecurity I've experienced over the course of my life, now seem a small price to pay for all that life has given me. What a gift to go on this journey to discover the answers to: Who am I?—A multi-dimensional being with six senses who's both a personality and an eternal Soul temporarily inhabiting a physical body; Why am I Here?—To experience the challenges and obstacles on earth and use them as opportunities to evolve and become a healing presence in the world; What's My Higher Purpose?—To identify the two or three emotions we came here to master, practice living their enlightened state, and master the contents of our Soul plan.

I look forward one day to crossing over and entering the Temple in the sky, knowing I did my best. I can hardly wait to sit with the Beings of Light to review my Soul plan, and to recognize and celebrate the level of enlightenment I achieved by facing, Soulercising, and transforming my challenges on earth.

I know that when I do cross over, Tam and Pete, Mom, Dad, and Jeanne, Bettye, and Honey and Janet—all my loved ones—will be there to greet me. But I'm in no rush to leave. I still have a lot of work to do here!

I also know that no matter who we are, no matter what happens to us or those we love, we have everything to live for. What a gift it is to value our challenges on earth and access the wisdom and guidance of our eternal Soul at every step of our journey; to feel a sense of personal victory through our emotional struggles each day.

What a privilege it is to be able to share these insights with other Soul Seekers and with those in our life who in the face of their own challenges and overwhelming emotions, strive to expand their light and fulfill their own higher purpose towards self-discovery and enlightenment.

The wisdom we seek resides within each of us in our very own Soul. And it resides in the Soul of everyone we know. Let's honor our Soul's brief time on earth and the mission we all set out to accomplish.

We hold the golden ticket to Soul consciousness in any moment of every blessed day—right here, right now, right within us. Let's find healing and insights in all aspects of life, from the mundane to even the most traumatic.

By doing so, we embody the strength and wisdom of our eternal Soul, evolve into higher states of being, and become a healing presence in the world.

May the light within and around us guide us on our path through life, always and forever.

Thank you!

Acknowledgements

I would like to sincerely acknowledge my mentors, to whom I am eternally grateful: Mrs. A., my high school principal, who took me under her wing and taught me the answers lie within; J. Krishnamurti whose extraordinary book *Freedom from the Known* taught me at 18 yrs. old to be a light to yourself during difficult times; Paramahansa Yogananda, whose teachings in *Autobiography of a Yogi* and the Self-Realization Fellowship (SRF) home study lessons initiated me at 20 yrs. old into the practices of Kriya Yoga and Meditation.

Also, to: Betty Bethards whose extraordinary teachings through the Inner Light Foundation validated my own remarkable experiences and taught me to be my own guru; and Dana Duryea whose spiritual seminars at the Foundation for Spiritual Development (FSD) showed me how to run energy.

I am also deeply grateful to all NeuroFit Marin clients, past and present, who've experienced the benefits of Soulercise first-hand in the NeuroFit Mind Fitness program. Your dedication and commitment to self-healing through NeuroFitness is bringing greater peace and contentment into the world, one Soul at a time.

I'm especially grateful to my mom, Vevie, whose enthusiasm and encouragement to pursue my vision kept me on the path; my dad, Bo, who taught me the art and practice of goal setting; my other mother, Jeannie, who supported me in achieving those goals; my sister, Debby, who graces my life with her love and friendship—I'm so thankful for you; my daughter Tamarin, whose miraculous after-death presence is a stunning verification that we are eternal beings; and my partner Rob, who brings the gift of laughter into my life. I love you all!

Finally, to Doug Childers whose pruning and polishing helped me illuminate the world of Spirit for my readers, and *the*BookDesigners for a cover that truly incarnates my spiritual vision. To everyone who helped make this book possible, I thank you from the bottom of my heart.

Thank you all!!!

About the Author

CINDY REYNOLDS is the founder of NeuroFit Marin, a center to "Cross-Train Your Brain." For the last 12 years, Cindy has built a Brain Fitness program that uses qEEG (quantitative Encephalopathy) Brain Mapping technology to identify the source of presenting symptoms and then applies cutting-edge NeuroTechnology to train your brain.

Inspired by personal tragedies from a young age, Cindy turned within on a journey that led to the discovery of our higher self within—our Soul. As a result, she also created the Mind Fitness program at NeuroFit called *Soulercise*—7 steps to exercise your Soul for peak performance during the challenges of daily life.

Cindy is available for speaking engagements and media/podcast interviews. To learn more about upcoming books, online programs, or to contact Cindy visit www.CindyReynolds.com. There you can also:

Get your free report, "Are you a Soul Seeker?"

Made in the USA
Monee, IL
28 January 2023

25734208R00142